POPE BENEDICT'S
DIVINE MERCY MANDATE

Pope Benedict's Divine Mercy Mandate

By David Came

MARIAN PRESS
STOCKBRIDGE MA 01263

PRO CHRISTO ET ECCLESIA

2011

Available from:
Marian Helpers Center
Stockbridge, MA 01263

Prayerline: 1-800-904-3823
Orderline: 1-800-462-7426
Website: www.marian.org

Imprimi potest:
Very Rev. Daniel Cambra, MIC
Provincial Superior
November 29, 2008

Library of Congress Catalog Number: 2008942142

ISBN: 978-1-59614-203-9

Cover Photo: CNS photo/Nancy Wiechec

Design of Cover: Mary Flannery
Design of Pages: Kathy Szpak

Editing and Proofreading:
Dan Valenti and Mary Flannery

Printed in the United States of America

*This book is dedicated to
His Holiness, Benedict XVI,
our Mercy Pope.*

Table of Contents

Introduction

Anyone who has studied the speeches, homilies, and writings of Pope Benedict XVI knows he is a deep thinker who chooses his words with care. So it was startling when at the close of the first World Apostolic Congress on Mercy in 2008, he called the participants to fulfill a Divine Mercy mandate:

> Yes, dear friends, the first World Congress on Divine Mercy ended this morning with the Eucharistic Celebration in St. Peter's Basilica. I thank the organizers, especially the Vicariate of Rome, and to all the participants I address my cordial greeting which now becomes a mandate: go forth and be witnesses of God's mercy, a source of hope for every person and for the whole world. May the Risen Lord be with you always! (*Regina Caeli* message, April 6, 2008).

Not only are these powerful words to the participants global in scope, but they bear the force and authority of a mandate. Mandate means "an authoritative command, order, or injunction;

a clear instruction, authorization, or direction" (*Webster's Third New International Dictionary*). In popular language, we might say that the Pope had just given the participants their marching orders as they prepared to leave Rome and return home — nearly 4,000 strong among 200 delegations from every corner of the globe.

I would argue, however, that Pope Benedict's mandate is not limited to the delegates who came to Rome. Remember that he was speaking at the conclusion of the first World Apostolic Congress on Mercy. So in the context of such an event representing the *universal* Church, surely his remarks are intended for all the faithful who desire to spread the Good News of God's mercy. Potentially, that includes everyone around the world who has embraced The Divine Mercy movement in the Church, or anyone who has experienced the healing touch of God's mercy and now wants to share it with others.

In considering what this mandate might mean to all the faithful who desire to implement it, I began to trace the thread of Divine Mercy throughout the papacy of Benedict. To my joy, I discovered what might be considered a papal program for what it means to "go forth and be witnesses of God's mercy" — fulfilling the mandate. Sharing these discoveries, which unfold chapter by chapter, is the purpose of this book. In fact, each chapter closes with a summary entitled "Fulfilling the Mandate."

It's important before we begin, though, to explain that Pope Benedict usually uses "God's mercy" and "Divine Mercy" interchangeably to refer to the mystery of God's mercy toward us as revealed in Sacred Scripture and Church Tradition. Consider, for example, his remarks on issuing his mandate. He opens them with mention of "the first World Congress on Divine Mercy" (even though the official name is the World Apostolic Congress on Mercy). Then he speaks of the call to "be witnesses of God's mercy." In both cases, he is speaking of the same reality, whether he calls it "God's mercy" or "Divine Mercy."

Now, in our day, Divine Mercy also refers to a particular message and forms of devotion given to St. Faustina by Jesus in the 1930s and recorded by her in her *Diary*. This message and the devotions associated with it call us to trust in Jesus as our merciful Savior, to receive His mercy, and share that mercy with others. It is as if God has put a spotlight on our world situation through St. Faustina, emphasizing Divine Mercy as an urgent message for our troubled times.

This message is based on the reality of God's mercy, rooted in Scripture and Tradition. In fact, it's worth highlighting that Cardinal Andrew Deskur — a close friend of Pope John Paul II — compared the *Diary of St. Faustina* to John Paul II's second encyclical, *Dives in Misericordia (Rich in Mercy)*, saying, "They draw their inspiration from the same source: namely, from the revelation of God and the teaching of Christ" (Original Preface to the Polish edition of the *Diary of St. Faustina*, 1981).

As a great apostle of Divine Mercy, Pope John Paul II embraced this message, especially when he declared the Second Sunday of Easter as Divine Mercy Sunday at the canonization of St. Faustina on April 30, 2000. In highlighting the urgency of The Divine Mercy message for our time, he even said of St. Faustina's canonization, "By this act I intend today to pass this message on to the new millennium." He also entrusted the world to Divine Mercy on August 17, 2002, in Lagiewniki, Poland, when he consecrated the International Shrine of The Divine Mercy there.

As we shall see, Pope Benedict is following John Paul II's lead in highlighting this message of Divine Mercy in our day. On September 28, 2008, for instance, he honored Fr.

Michael Sopocko, the newly beatified spiritual director and confessor of St. Faustina, for his role in guiding the religious sister and mystic.

"At his suggestion," Pope Benedict said, "[Sister] Faustina described her mystical experiences and apparitions of the merciful Jesus in her well-known *Diary*. Thanks to his efforts, the image with the words, 'Jesus, I trust in you,' was painted and transmitted to the world. This Servant of God became known as a zealous priest, teacher and promoter of the Divine Mercy devotion."

Further, Pope Benedict took this occasion to salute John Paul II when he remarked, "My beloved Predecessor, the Servant of God John Paul II most certainly rejoices in this beatification in the Father's house. He is the one who entrusted the world to Divine Mercy. That is why I repeat his wish, 'May the God who is rich in mercy bless all of you'" (*Angelus* message, September 28, 2008, translation from the Polish).

With all this in mind, let's begin to see what Pope Benedict's Divine Mercy mandate involves and how we can fulfill it. Interestingly, our first discovery involves a gift that Benedict received when he was elected Pope. Not surprisingly, the man behind the gift was none other than John Paul II.

CHAPTER ONE

'A Gift of Divine Mercy'

On April 20, 2005, in his first message as Pope, Benedict XVI spoke with remarkable candor about his apprehension upon being elected. It's telling that in the midst of what he called "contrasting emotions," he expressed "deep gratitude for a gift of Divine Mercy." Further, the new Pontiff emphasized how he believed that this gift had been obtained for him through the intercession of his predecessor, John Paul II:

> At this time, side by side in my heart, I feel two contrasting emotions. On the one hand, a sense of inadequacy and human apprehension as I face the responsibility for the universal Church, entrusted to me yesterday as Successor of the Apostle Peter in this See of Rome. On the other, I have a lively feeling of profound gratitude to God who, as the liturgy makes us sing, never leaves his flock untended but leads it down the ages under the guidance of those whom

© CNS photo by Nancy Wiechec

Pope Benedict XVI greets the faithful in St. Peter's Square at his election on April 19, 2005: On April 20, 2005, during his first message as Pope, he spoke of his "deep gratitude for a gift of Divine Mercy" that he attributed to the intercession of his predecessor, John Paul II.

he himself has chosen as the Vicars of his Son and has made shepherds of the flock (cf. *Preface of Apostles I*).

Dear friends, this deep gratitude for a gift of Divine Mercy is uppermost in my heart in spite of all. And I consider it a special grace which my Venerable Predecessor, John Paul II, has obtained for me. I seem to feel his strong hand clasping mine; I seem to see his smiling eyes and hear his words, at this moment addressed specifically to me, "Do not be afraid!"

Predisposed to Receive the Gift

What exactly was the context for the new Pope receiving "a gift of Divine Mercy"?

To answer this question, we should consider Pope John Paul II's *Regina Caeli* message for Divine Mercy Sunday 2005 that was shared with the faithful in St. Peter's Square on April 3, 2005, the day after his death, which was Mercy Sunday. We should also reflect on then Joseph Cardinal Ratzinger's words in his April 8, 2005, funeral homily for John Paul II. When we do, we discover *why* Pope Benedict was predisposed to receive this gift when he became Pope.

First, before we consider John Paul's *Regina Caeli* message, it's important to realize that he was seriously ill and surely knew that this would probably be his last annual Divine Mercy Sunday message to the Church and the world. Further, it's likely the future Pope Benedict, then Cardinal Ratzinger — as John Paul's longtime prefect of the Congregation for the Doctrine of the Faith who had met with him weekly for nearly 24 years — was cognizant of all this and reflected deeply on these inspiring words after the death of his beloved Pope:

> As a gift to humanity, which sometimes seems bewildered and overwhelmed by the power of evil, selfishness and fear, the Risen Lord offers his love that pardons, reconciles and reopens hearts to love. It is a love that converts hearts and gives peace. How much the world needs to understand and accept Divine Mercy!
>
> Lord, [you] who reveal the Father's love by your death and Resurrection, we believe in you and confidently repeat to you today: Jesus, I trust in you, have mercy upon us and upon the whole world (*Regina Caeli* message of Pope

John Paul II, prepared for Divine Mercy Sunday, April 3, 2005).

Notice how John Paul talks of the Risen Lord offering "a gift to humanity" and emphasizes how humanity is sometimes "bewildered and overwhelmed" by fear. Compare this to Pope Benedict's mention in his first message as Pontiff of his own "sense of inadequacy and human apprehension." Further, we see a striking correspondence between John Paul's enthusiastic devotion to Divine Mercy in declaring, "How much the world needs to understand and accept Divine Mercy!" and Benedict describing in endearing terms a personal encounter with John Paul as he received "a gift of Divine Mercy": "I seem to feel his strong hand clasping mine; I seem to see his smiling eyes and hear his words, at this moment addressed specifically to me, 'Do not be afraid!'"

Finally, in his last Divine Mercy Sunday message, John Paul speaks of humanity being "overwhelmed by the power of evil." This is a theme that then Cardinal Ratzinger picks up in his homily at John Paul II's funeral Mass at which he presided as dean of the College of Cardinals:

> [Pope John Paul II] interpreted for us the paschal mystery as a mystery of Divine

Mercy. In his last book, he wrote: The limit imposed upon evil "is ultimately Divine Mercy" (*Memory and Identity*, pp. 54-55). And reflecting on the assassination attempt, he said, "In sacrificing himself for us all, Christ gave a new meaning to suffering, opening up a new dimension, a new order: the order of love. ... It is this suffering which burns and consumes evil with the flame of love and draws forth even from sin a great flowering of good" (pp. 167-168).

This key insight of John Paul's about Divine Mercy imposing a limit upon evil — especially as expressed in the paschal mystery of Christ's suffering — was most likely on Cardinal Ratzinger's mind not only at the funeral but in the days leading up to his election as Pope. It surely helped sustain him during his mourning for John Paul and then helped make him receptive to a gift of Divine Mercy upon his own election.

To shed more light on this gift and its personal connection for Pope Benedict with John Paul, it's also helpful to consider an interview of Pope Benedict conducted by Polish State Television (TVP) to mark the occasion of the

Polish Parliament in 2005 establishing October 16th (the day Cardinal Karol Wojtyla of Krakow was elected Pope) as Pope John Paul II Day in Poland.

The Internet news service Zenit reported that when Pope Benedict was asked by the Polish State Television interviewer to highlight "the most significant moments of the Pontificate of John Paul II," he mentioned among the late Pope's main legacies that "he created a new awareness of the greatness of Divine Mercy."

Interestingly, as we have just seen, John Paul's "awareness of the greatness of Divine Mercy" certainly had a profound impact on Benedict himself, both when he presided at John Paul's funeral and then at his own election as Pope.

But there's more. When the interviewer asked Pope Benedict if he continues "to feel the presence of John Paul II," his response is reminiscent of the personal tone of his comments about John Paul during his first message as his successor. It's almost as if he is reading off the same page several months later:

> Certainly ... the Pope is always close to me through his writings: I hear him and I see him speaking, so I can keep up a con-

tinuous dialogue with him. He is always speaking to me through his writings. ... So I can continue my conversations with the Holy Father. This nearness to him isn't limited to words and texts, because behind the texts I hear the Pope himself. A man who goes to the Lord doesn't disappear: I believe that someone who goes to the Lord comes even closer to us, and I feel he is close to me and that I am close to the Lord. I am near the Pope and now he helps me to be near the Lord, and I try to enter this atmosphere of prayer, of love for our Lord, for Our Lady, and I entrust myself to his prayers. So there is a permanent dialogue, and we're close to each other in a new way, in a very deep way.

In sum, we see that, after his death, John Paul has continued to speak to Benedict through his writings and that "behind the texts," John Paul continues to inspire Benedict. Further, Benedict's relationship with John Paul even deepened spiritually after the latter's death and must have been particularly intense in the days before Benedict's election — thus setting the stage for the new Pontiff's receptivity to "a gift of Divine Mercy" through the intercession of John Paul II. Their weekly meetings of nearly 24 years as Pontiff and prefect had borne fruit.

'A Great Gift of Divine Mercy,' 80 Years of Life

Two years later, Pope Benedict mentions his gratitude for "a great gift of Divine Mercy to have been granted birth and rebirth" upon celebrating his 80th birthday. He includes his rebirth in his remarks, since he was baptized with the first water of Easter on Holy Saturday, the very day he was born.

The occasion is significant. It is April 15, 2007, which is Divine Mercy Sunday that year, and he chooses to celebrate his birthday on Mercy Sunday even though his birthday is on April 16.

In his homily for the occasion, Pope Benedict seems almost to take up where he had left off with his comments about John Paul and "a gift of Divine Mercy" two years earlier at his election. Read carefully and compare these words with those in the last section:

> Two years ago now, after the First Vespers of this Feast, John Paul II ended his earthly life. In dying, he entered the light

of Divine Mercy, of which, beyond death and starting from God, he now speaks to us in a new way.

Have faith, he tells us, in Divine Mercy! Become day after day men and women of God's mercy. Mercy is the garment of light which the Lord has given to us in Baptism. We must not allow this light to be extinguished; on the contrary, it must grow within us every day and thus bring to the world God's glad tidings.

In these days illumined in particular by the light of Divine Mercy, a coincidence occurs that is significant to me: I can look back on over 80 years of life.

The Pope then continues in a more personal vein:

I have always considered it a great gift of Divine Mercy to have been granted birth and rebirth, so to speak, on the same day, in the sign of the beginning of Easter. Thus, I was born as a member of my own family and of the great family of God on the same day.

As Benedict celebrates the gift of Divine

Mercy in his own rebirth through Baptism, observe in particular how he speaks of mercy as "the garment of light which the Lord has given to us in Baptism." He is saying that the great dignity we have all been given in Baptism as children of God is a result of God's great mercy in saving us from our sins. He encourages all of us who are baptized to let this light of mercy from our Baptism "grow within us every day."

Pope Benedict develops this theme further for all of us later in his homily when he sums up, "Birth and rebirth, an earthly family and the great family of God: this is the great gift of God's multiple mercies, the foundation of which supports us."

But he doesn't end there. No, he encourages us to be aware of "God's multiple mercies" every day of our life. "God's mercy accompanies us daily," he says. "To be able to perceive his mercy it suffices to have a heart that is alert. We are excessively inclined to notice only the daily effort that has been imposed upon as children of Adam."

Here, the Holy Father is reminding us that as children of the light who now live in Christ, we need to grow in daily awareness of "God's multiple mercies." We must ask for spiritual sight to recognize the mercies of the Lord and express our gratitude to God for them every day.

In responding to this call, the challenge for me is that I tend to develop tunnel vision when I am under the press of deadlines as an editor or a writer. All I can see at such times is the immediate goal of finishing an issue of the magazine I edit or writing a particular article. At such times, I can fail to appreciate fully the natural beauty that surrounds me when I arrive to work on Eden Hill in Stockbridge, Massachusetts. I can miss the wonder of my daily participation in weekday Mass at Our Lady of Mercy Oratory here at the Marian Helpers Center.

What about you?

All of us — as baptized children of God — have received "a great gift of Divine Mercy." In that light, our Holy Father is inviting us to open the eyes of our heart in order to receive it. It is expressed daily in "God's multiple mercies" toward us. But if we don't keep our eyes on the Lord and His mercies, we become weighed down by our sinful tendencies as children of Adam. As a result, our spiritual vision becomes clouded, and we miss the blessing — the sense of gratitude and joy — that God intended for us.

But there's more to the gift we have received, as we shall see in our next chapter.

FULFILLING THE MANDATE

Before we can go forth as witnesses of God's mercy, we must receive a gift of Divine Mercy ourselves. It is fundamentally the great gift of our Baptism in Christ and is then expressed in the many mercies of the Lord, which we experience every day when we keep open the eyes of our heart to perceive them. Let us pray through the intercession of Blessed John Paul II for the grace to grow daily in an "awareness of the greatness of Divine Mercy." It's a lesson Pope Benedict himself has learned from his predecessor in the Chair of Peter.

CHAPTER TWO

'Mercy, Central Nucleus of the Gospel Message'

What exactly are the contents of the gift of Divine Mercy that each of us has received by virtue of our Baptism?

During his more than six years as Pope, Benedict has shown us that the essential content of the gift is nothing less than our salvation through the paschal mystery — the Passion, death, and Resurrection of our Lord and Savior Jesus Christ. Divine Mercy is at the heart of the Gospel itself, core to the Christian faith.

In his message for Divine Mercy Sunday 2006 — his first as Pope — he stressed that "Divine Mercy is not a secondary devotion but an integral dimension of Christian faith and prayer" (*Regina Caeli* message, April 23, 2006). On Divine Mercy Sunday 2008, he went so far as to say, "Mercy is the central nucleus of the Gospel message; it is the very name of God, the Face with which he revealed himself in the Old Testament and fully in Jesus Christ, the incarnation of creative and

© Joe Romagnano

Pope Benedict XVI greets the faithful at Holy Mass on September 14, 2008, during his pastoral visit to Lourdes, France: It was the feast of the Exaltation of the Holy Cross, and Pope Benedict in his homily referred to the Cross as "a source of life, pardon, mercy, a sign of reconciliation and hope."

redemptive Love" (*Regina Caeli* message, March 30, 2008).

But I'm getting ahead of myself. Let's look in more depth at what Benedict has said about God's mercy and the paschal mystery — especially in his Lenten and Divine Mercy Sunday messages.

Lent and Good Friday: Mercy and the Paschal Mystery

What's the connection between the compassionate "gaze" of Christ and human development? What does it mean to be "infected" by mercy? How is almsgiving more than mere philanthropy? These are some of the questions Pope Benedict addresses in his Lenten and Good Friday messages as he develops how mercy is at the heart of the paschal mystery.

The Pope opens his Lenten message for 2006 — which is devoted to the urgent need for human development — with these words that evoke an image of God's ever-flowing mercy, "Lent is a privileged time of interior pilgrimage towards him who is the fount of mercy." He speaks of a pilgrimage in which God Himself "accompanies us through the desert of our poverty, sustaining us on the way towards the intense joy of Easter."

After describing the difficulties of journeying through the desert, the Holy Father reveals "mercy" as the inspiration of his Lenten message and then makes the connection with the paschal mystery in presenting his main point on human development:

> Yet, even in the desolation of misery, loneliness, violence and hunger that indiscriminately afflict children, adults and the elderly, God does not allow darkness to prevail. In fact, in the words of my beloved Predecessor, Pope John Paul II, there is a "divine limit imposed upon evil," namely, mercy (*Memory and Identity*, pp. 15ff.). It is with these thoughts in mind that I have chosen as my theme for this message the Gospel text: "Jesus, at the sight of the crowds, was moved with pity" (Mt 9:36).

> In this light, I would like to pause and reflect upon an issue much debated today: the question of development. Even now, the compassionate "gaze" of Christ continues to fall upon individuals and peoples. He watches them, knowing that the divine "plan" includes their call

to salvation. Jesus knows the perils that put this plan at risk, and he is moved with pity for the crowds. He chooses to defend them from the wolves even at the cost of his own life. The gaze of Jesus embraces individuals and multitudes, and he brings them all before the Father, offering himself as a sacrifice for expiation.

Enlightened by this Paschal truth, the Church knows that if we are to promote development in its fullness, our own "gaze" upon mankind has to be measured against that of Christ.

Pope Benedict is saying that meeting the material and social needs of the poor is not enough. They need God's mercy to overcome evil. We must seek their spiritual welfare, being compassionate toward them like Christ, who laid down His life for them as the Good Shepherd of their souls.

He then invokes "the examples of the saints and the long history of the Church's missionary activity" in helping others "find God in the merciful face of Christ": "[The saints] know that he who does not give God gives too little; as Blessed Teresa of Calcutta frequently observed, the worst poverty is not to know Christ. Therefore, we must help others to find God in the merciful face of Christ."

On Good Friday, April 14, 2006, Pope Benedict again emphasizes mercy, referring to it as the "limit on evil." During his reflection for the Way of the Cross at the Colosseum, he says, "The Way of the Cross is the way of mercy that puts a limit on evil: this is what we learned from Pope John Paul II. It is the way of mercy, hence, the way of salvation. Thus, we are invited to take the way of mercy and, with Jesus, put a limit on evil."

When the Holy Father closes in prayer, he even uses the jarring analogy of infection to emphasize how much all of us need to catch mercy: "Let us pray to the Lord to help us be 'infected' by his mercy."

For Lent 2007, Pope Benedict's theme is the Scripture passage, "They shall look on him whom they have pierced" (Jn 19:37). He weaves in mercy by bringing us to the foot of the Cross and then talking of "our trustful abandonment to the merciful embrace of the Father."

"It is in the mystery of the Cross that the overwhelming power of the Heavenly Father's mercy is revealed in all its fullness," the Pope said. "In order to win back the love of his creature, he accepted to pay a very high price: the Blood of his Only Begotten Son."

In that context, the Pope says that the Lenten call is ultimately one of abandonment to the Father, following the example of Christ: "In the Lenten journey, memorial of our Baptism, we are exhorted to come out of ourselves in order to open ourselves in trustful abandonment to the merciful embrace of the Father."

In Lent 2008, Pope Benedict focuses on almsgiving as a work of mercy for Lent. His key Scripture is: "Christ made himself poor for you" (2 Cor 8:9). The Holy Father opens his message:

> Each year, Lent offers us a providential opportunity to deepen the meaning and value of our Christian lives, and it stimulates us to rediscover the mercy of God so that we, in turn, become more merciful toward our brothers and sisters.

He explains how almsgiving as a work of mercy, which the Church encourages during Lent, is much more than philanthropy. In fact, it is linked to the paschal mystery as our imitation of Christ and should be done in secret, so we are not seeking "human recognition" for our work of mercy:

Almsgiving, according to the Gospel, is not mere philanthropy: rather it is a concrete expression of charity, a theological virtue that demands interior conversion to love of God and neighbor, in imitation of Jesus Christ, who, dying on the Cross, gave his entire self for us. ... There is little use in giving one's personal goods to others if it leads to a heart puffed up in vainglory: for this reason, the one, who knows that God "sees in secret" and in secret will reward, does not seek human recognition for works of mercy.

In almsgiving, then, we are not simply writing out a check and putting it into the collection basket. We are called to enter into the paschal mystery by pouring ourselves out in love of God and those in need. And we are told to keep our almsgiving secret, looking for no reward or attention in this life.

Divine Mercy Sunday: Mercy and the Paschal Mystery

I opened this chapter by sharing some amazing things that Pope Benedict said in his Divine Mercy Sunday messages. Here are some others. In one message, he speaks of Christ as "a wounded God" and of the implications for us. In another, he talks of the "merciful love" of God "show[ing] itself through the sacraments ... and in works of charity."

Getting at the meaning of these statements involves some heavy lifting, but stay with me. It's well worth the effort.

On Divine Mercy Sunday, April 23, 2006, Benedict states in his *Regina Caeli* message that based on the magisterium of Pope John Paul II: "Divine Mercy is not a secondary devotion but an integral dimension of Christian faith and prayer." It's no accident that this strong statement came during his first Mercy Sunday as Pope and only a year after the death of Pope John Paul II.

He also connects Divine Mercy and the sacred wounds in the glorified body of the Risen Christ, saying, "Those sacred wounds in his hands, in his feet and in his side are an inexhaustible source of faith, hope and love from which each one can draw, especially the souls who thirst the most for Divine Mercy."

Notice how the wounds of the Risen Christ are presented as the source of life-giving Divine Mercy, especially for souls who recognize their need for it.

In a marvelous way, Benedict then takes up where he left off in 2006, developing the wounds of Christ further in his homily on Divine Mercy Sunday, April 15, 2007:

> The Lord took his wounds with him to eternity. He is a wounded God; he let himself be injured through his love for us. His wounds are a sign that he understands and allows himself to be wounded out of love for us.
>
> These wounds of his: how tangible they are to us in the history of our time! Indeed, time and again, he allows himself to be wounded for our sake. What certainty of his mercy, what consolation do his wounds mean for us! ... And what a duty they are for us, the duty to allow ourselves in turn to be wounded for him!

These powerful words of our Holy Father are enough to leave you speechless. He is saying that since Christ brought His glorified body with its wounds into eternity, He now reigns as a wounded God. His wounds are a tangible sign that He understands our plight, and even now, in ways we can't fathom, He allows Himself to be wounded out of love for us.

Further, the wounds of our Lord give us the certainty of His mercy and can be a great source of consolation to us in our trials. Finally, His example of woundedness for us impels us to allow ourselves to be wounded out of love for Him and others. It provides meaning to our own sufferings as we share in the Lord's redemptive love for the world.

After these stunning paragraphs, consider this chock-filled statement on mercy by Pope Benedict during his *Regina Caeli* message on Divine Mercy Sunday, March 30, 2008. It reads like a "five-star" message that lays out the centrality of Divine Mercy for the Gospel, the life of the Church, and the peace and wellbeing of the world:

> Indeed, mercy is the central nucleus of the Gospel message; it is the very name of God, the Face with which he revealed himself in the Old Covenant and fully in Jesus Christ, the incarnation of creative and redemptive Love. May this merciful love also shine on the face of the Church and show itself through the sacraments, in particular that of Reconciliation, and in works of charity, both communitarian and individual. May all that the Church

says and does manifest the mercy God feels for man, and therefore for us. When the Church has to recall an unrecognized truth or a betrayed good, she always does so impelled by merciful love, so that men and women may have life and have it abundantly (cf. Jn 10:10). From Divine Mercy, which brings peace to hearts, genuine peace flows into the world, peace between different peoples, cultures and religions.

Let's see if we can parse this meaty statement along the lines of the Gospel, the Church, and the world.

The Gospel: Mercy is at the center of the Gospel message, the source of its dynamism, revealing to us the very name of God Himself. It can be traced in the Old Covenant and is realized fully in Jesus Christ, who is Divine Mercy Incarnate and who saved us by His Passion, death, and Resurrection.

The Church: In Christ, this merciful love is manifested through the sacramental life of His Church and the works of mercy that are done through her members. As such, the Church is called to show forth God's mercy to all men and women. Motivated by merciful love, the Church always defends the truth and the good for the life of souls.

The World: Only Divine Mercy can bring genuine peace to the human heart and the whole world, including "peace between different peoples, cultures and religions."

Passover and the Cross at Lourdes: Mercy and the Paschal Mystery

There were two other occasions, both in 2008, on which Pope Benedict highlighted mercy at the heart of the paschal mystery.

On April 17, 2008, during his pastoral visit to the U.S., he presented a message to the Jewish community in America on the feast of *Pesach* (Passover). In his message, he stressed the integral relationship between the Jewish *Pesach* and, for Christians, "the Passover of Christ's death and Resurrection":

> Christians and Jews share [the hope of freedom and redemption through the Covenant]; we are in fact, as the prophets say, "prisoners of hope" (Zech 9:12). This bond permits us Christians to celebrate alongside you, though in our own way, the Passover of Christ's death and

Resurrection, which we see as inseparable from your own, for Jesus himself said, "Salvation is from the Jews" (Jn 4:22). Our Easter and your *Pesach*, while distinct and different, unite us in our common hope centered on God and his mercy.

The Pope is saying that both the Jews' liberation through Moses from slavery in Egypt and our liberation through Christ from the bondage of sin, death, and the devil come from the same source: God's mercy.

In that light, he invites both the Jewish and Christian communities to remember "God's mercies" during their festive celebrations of *Pesach* and Easter, with an eye on the "shared hope for peace," especially in the Middle East and the Holy Land:

Naturally, our shared hope for peace in the world embraces the Middle East and the Holy Land in particular. May the memory of God's mercies, which Jews and Christians celebrate at this festive time, inspire all those responsible for the future of that region — where the events surrounding God's revelation actually took place — to new efforts, and especially to new attitudes and a new purification of hearts!

Then, on September 14, 2008, during his homily at Lourdes to celebrate the 150th anniversary of the Blessed Virgin Mary's apparitions there, he highlighted the mystery of the Cross since it was the feast of the Exaltation of the Cross. "By his Cross we are saved," the Holy Father said, referring to the Cross of Christ. "The instrument of torture which, on Good Friday, manifested God's judgment on the world has become a source of life, pardon, mercy, a sign of reconciliation and hope."

Just as Pope Benedict had called the Way of the Cross "the way of mercy" on Good Friday in 2006, here he is saying in 2008 that the Cross of Christ, among other things, has become "a source of mercy."

The Conversation Continues

We have seen, then, that throughout his papacy, Pope Benedict has emphasized that the mercy of God is right at the heart of the Passion, death, and Resurrection of Jesus Christ, the source of our salvation. It is not a secondary or optional element. Indeed, it is the source of the Church's life and the hope for peace in our troubled world. This is the essential content of the gift of Divine

Mercy that each of us received at Baptism.

But there's more. This emphasis by Pope Benedict is not his alone. It came to him through the legacy of his predecessor, Pope John Paul II. At Pope John Paul II's funeral Mass on April 8, 2005, then Cardinal Ratzinger himself said in his homily, "[John Paul II] interpreted the paschal mystery as a mystery of Divine Mercy." Benedict then used similar words as Pope in his homily on Divine Mercy Sunday, April 15, 2007, "The Holy Father, John Paul II, wanted this Sunday to be celebrated as the Feast of Divine Mercy: in the word, 'mercy,' he summed up and interpreted anew for our time the whole mystery of Redemption."

Remember from the last chapter, Pope Benedict's interview on Polish television in 2005. Perhaps this is an example of the "permanent dialogue" that the Pope talked about between himself and John Paul. Perhaps the paschal mystery and Divine Mercy have been among their topics of spiritual conversation.

On a personal level, we should enter into a conversation of our own — one of prayer with the Lord Jesus Christ, thanking Him for the great gift of His mercy in saving us from our sins through His Passion, death, and Resurrection. After all, Christ went to the Cross out of love for each one of us — to pay the penalty for all our sins. How wondrous is His great love and mercy toward us!

Let's take some time right now to do just that.

Moving on, in our next chapter, we'll see various ways in which Pope Benedict is carrying on the Divine Mercy legacy of John Paul II. The conversation between the two of them seems to be continuing. Let's listen in.

FULFILLING THE MANDATE

The greatest gift of Divine Mercy that each of us has been given is our salvation through the Passion, death, and Resurrection of Jesus Christ. This is the Good News of the Gospel that we are impelled to share as witnesses of God's mercy. This is the main reason why God's mercy is "a source of hope for every person and for the whole world," as Pope Benedict puts it in his mandate. If we want to spread Divine Mercy, according to the teaching of our Holy Father and the Church, this Gospel of Mercy must be our central focus. We should always remember that we are not only called to proclaim it but to live it ourselves.

CHAPTER THREE

Making John Paul II's Divine Mercy Legacy Our Own

Pope Benedict is carrying on, even solidifying, the Divine Mercy legacy of his predecessor, Blessed John Paul II. He understands and emphasizes that God's mercy is expressed most fully in connection with the paschal mystery of our salvation. Indeed, as we saw in our last chapter, the Holy Father tells us with clarity on Divine Mercy Sunday 2008 that "mercy [is] the central nucleus of the Gospel message."

In this and other ways, the Pope is serving as a guarantor of John Paul's Divine Mercy legacy. He is helping us make this important legacy of mercy our own. We saw this especially in his pastoral visit to Poland in 2006, and we have seen it on each Divine Mercy Sunday that he has celebrated as Pope.

L'Osservatore Romano

On April 30, 2000, in St. Peter's Square, Pope John Paul II reads the words of canonization for St. Faustina: In this chapter, we will see how Pope Benedict XVI has repeatedly linked The Divine Mercy message given to St. Faustina and the pontificate of John Paul II. For Benedict, St. Faustina is the Divine Mercy mystic and Blessed John Paul II is her interpreter. Further, in his statements, Pope Benedict hails both St. Faustina and Blessed John Paul II as great apostles of Divine Mercy and even as prophets of mercy for our troubled times.

Following in the Footsteps
of the 'Great Mercy Pope'

When Pope Benedict arrived at the Warsaw Airport on May 25, 2006, for his pastoral visit to John Paul II's homeland, he set the tone, saying, "I have very much wanted to make this visit to the native land and people of my beloved Predecessor, the Servant of God John Paul II. I have come to follow in the footsteps of his life, from his boyhood until his departure for the memorable conclave of 1978." In essence, the Pope was coming to celebrate the life of his predecessor with those who knew him best, his beloved countrymen.

In following "in the footsteps" of the man many have hailed as the "Great Mercy Pope," his pastoral visit naturally had to include The Divine Mercy Shrine in Lagiewniki, Poland. He knew it was where St. Faustina, the visionary associated with The Divine Mercy message, lived and was buried. Benedict knew Pope John Paul II himself dedicated the shrine in 2002 and also entrusted the world to Divine Mercy there. In fact, when he visited Lagiewniki on May 27, 2006, Benedict hearkened back to John Paul's entrustment when he repeated the latter's words on that special occasion:

As Pope John Paul II said in this place: "The Cross is the most profound bowing down of the Divinity towards man ... the Cross is like a touch of eternal love on the most painful wounds of humanity's earthly existence" (August 17, 2002).

It's no surprise, then, that Pope Benedict said in his May 31, 2006, General Audience that a stop at the shrine in Lagiewniki "could not have been omitted from my itinerary."

In recalling the visit to the shrine during his General Audience, Benedict spoke of John Paul "echo[ing] and interpret[ing]" "a message of trust for humanity" that St. Faustina received from the Risen Christ:

It was here at the neighboring convent that Sr. Faustina Kowalska, contemplating the shining wounds of the Risen Christ, received a message of trust for humanity which John Paul II echoed and interpreted and which really is a central message precisely for our time: Mercy as God's power, as a divine barrier against the evil of the world.

We will see time and again how Pope Benedict has linked The Divine Mercy message given to St. Faustina and the pontificate of John Paul II, the Great Mercy Pope.

Divine Mercy Sunday: A Keystone of John Paul II's Legacy

Pope Benedict is most incisive in making the connection between St. Faustina, the Divine Mercy mystic, and her interpreter, John Paul II, in his Divine Mercy Sunday messages. It makes perfect sense since Pope John Paul II chose the occasion of St. Faustina's canonization on April 30, 2000, to declare the Second Sunday of Easter as Divine Mercy Sunday for the universal Church. The Great Mercy Pope also died on April 2, 2005, at 9:37 p.m., which was the vigil of Divine Mercy Sunday that year.

Consider these strong Mercy Sunday statements of Pope Benedict that connect the mystic and her interpreter. On Divine Mercy Sunday, April 23, 2006, he noted in his *Regina Caeli* that "the Servant of God John Paul II, highlighting the spiritual experience of a humble Sister, St. Faustina Kowalska, desired that the Sunday after Easter be dedicated in a special way to Divine Mercy; and Providence disposed that he would die precisely on the eve of this day in the hands of Divine Mercy."

Then, on Divine Mercy Sunday 2008, in his *Regina Caeli* message, Benedict goes further by linking both John Paul and St. Faustina as apostles of Divine Mercy. You almost get a sense of John Paul taking up where Faustina left off in spreading the Good News of God's mercy:

Like Sr. Faustina, John Paul II in his turn made himself an apostle of Divine Mercy. In the evening of the unforgettable Saturday, April 2, 2005, when he closed his eyes on this world, it was precisely the eve of the Second Sunday of Easter and many people noted the rare coincidence that combined the Marian dimension — the first Saturday of the month — and the dimension of Divine Mercy. This was in fact the core of John Paul II's long and multi-faceted Pontificate. The whole of his mission at the service of the truth about God and man and of peace in the world is summed up in this declaration, as he himself said in Krakow-Lagiewniki in 2002 when he inaugurated the large Shrine of Divine Mercy: "Apart from the mercy of God there is no source of hope for mankind." John Paul II's message, like

St. Faustina's, thus leads back to the Face of Christ, a supreme revelation of God's mercy. Constant contemplation of this Face is the legacy he bequeathed to us which we joyfully welcome and make our own.

This statement is extraordinary for its richness and implications, but let's focus for our purposes here on only the last couple of sentences. First, notice Benedict speaks of how "John Paul II's message, like St. Faustina's, ... leads back to the Face of Christ, a supreme revelation of God's mercy." Upon reading this, anyone familiar with The Divine Mercy message and devotion would immediately think of The Divine Mercy image, which is an image of the Risen Christ, with glorious rays of healing streaming forth from His pierced Heart. And as the merciful Savior instructed St. Faustina, this image should be venerated precisely on Divine Mercy Sunday to inspire the faithful to trust in the Lord Jesus and to perform works of mercy out of love for Him. It is no coincidence, then, that this statement of Pope Benedict came on Mercy Sunday.

More relevant to our point here, Pope Benedict talks of "the legacy [John Paul II] bequeathed to us which we joyfully welcome and make our own." In effect, as the current Holy Father, Pope Benedict is saying that we are carrying on John Paul's Divine Mercy legacy and making it our own. We are even "joyfully welcom[ing]" it as our own. John Paul's legacy of mercy, then, is an inheritance to the whole Church — an inheritance we are called to embrace.

'God's Mercy ... a Privileged Key' to Interpreting John Paul II's Life

A signal moment for Pope Benedict in helping the Church understand and appreciate John Paul's legacy of mercy came on April 2, 2008, during Holy Mass on the third anniversary of the Great Mercy Pope's death. In his homily, Pope Benedict examines his predecessor's life through the lens of Divine Mercy to explain why it is essential to understanding John Paul's papacy. Once again, Benedict presents St. Faustina as a pivotal figure for John Paul. This time, he describes her as a "prophetic messenger of Divine Mercy" amidst "the terrible tragedies of the 20th century" that Karol Wojtyla (the future Pope John Paul II) and his Polish compatriots experienced, alluding especially to the horrors of World War II:

God's mercy, as [Pope John Paul II] himself said, is a privileged key to the interpretation of his Pontificate. He wanted the message of God's merciful love to be made known to all and urged the faithful to witness to it (cf. Homily at Krakow-Lagiewniki, August 17, 2002). This is why he raised to the honor of the altars Sr. Faustina Kowalska, a humble Sister who, through a mysterious divine plan, became a prophetic messenger of Divine Mercy. The Servant of God John Paul II had known and personally experienced the terrible tragedies of the 20th century and for a long time wondered what could stem the tide of evil. The answer could only be found in God's love. In fact, only Divine Mercy is able to impose limitations on evil; only the almighty love of God can defeat the tyranny of the wicked and the destructive power of selfishness and hate. For this reason, during his last visit to Poland, he said on his return to the land of his birth: "Apart from the mercy of God there is no other source of hope for mankind" (Homily at Krakow-Lagiewniki, August 17, 2002).

In this homily, we can almost hear Benedict talking with John Paul about his life when he observes that "for a long time" Karol Wojtyla had "wondered what could stem the tide of evil," based upon his own tragic experiences in Poland. Benedict is then saying that the prophetic revelations of St. Faustina provided the key to opposing evil for Wojtyla, so that on his last visit to his homeland, as Pope John Paul II, he could confidently proclaim to the Church and the world, "Apart from the mercy of God there is no other source of hope for mankind."

Further, Benedict closes his homily with a remarkable statement that leaves no doubt that he has taken up his predecessor's "priceless spiritual legacy" and is calling the Church to follow John Paul II's "teaching and example":

> And while we offer the redeeming Sacrifice for [John Paul II's] chosen soul, let us pray to him to continue to intercede from Heaven for each one of us, especially for me whom Providence called to take up his priceless spiritual legacy. The Church, following his teaching and example, faithfully continues without compromising in her evangelizing mission

and never ceases to spread Christ's merciful love, a source of true peace for the whole world.

'Beloved John Paul II, a Great Apostle of Divine Mercy' for Our Time

It's significant that Benedict chooses to highlight the Divine Mercy legacy of John Paul II not only on special occasions but during his ordinary teaching office as Pope. In his September 16, 2007, *Angelus* message, for instance, he talks about "the three parables of mercy" in that Sunday's Gospel reading from Luke 15. Then he points to the significance in our time of John Paul II's "strong proclamation and witness of God's mercy":

> In our time, humanity needs a strong proclamation and witness of God's mercy. Beloved John Paul II, a great apostle of Divine Mercy, prophetically intuited this urgent pastoral need. He dedicated his second Encyclical to it and throughout his Pontificate made himself the missionary of God's love to all peoples.

> After the tragic events of September 11, 2001, which darkened the dawn of the

third millennium, he invited Christians and people of good will to believe that God's mercy is stronger than all evil, and that only in the Cross of Christ is the world's salvation found.

There are three things worth noticing about Pope Benedict's remarks here. In arresting language, he describes John Paul in his own right as "a great apostle of Divine Mercy," who "prophetically intuited [the] urgent pastoral need" for God's mercy in our age. This is akin to what Pope Benedict said in our last section about St. Faustina when he described her as a "prophetic messenger of Divine Mercy" in helping the younger Karol Wojtyla come to terms with his experience of evil in his homeland. Now, John Paul II is being hailed as a prophet of mercy in his own right.

Second, Pope Benedict mentions how his predecessor "dedicated his second Encyclical" to God's mercy. He is referring to *Dives in Misericordia (Rich in Mercy)* in which John Paul II demonstrated how God the Father is "rich in mercy" through a masterful exposition of Scripture, especially the Gospel parable of the prodigal son. And this is the main parable from Luke 15 that Benedict himself had just com-

In Honor of the Holy Family

O God, Heavenly Father, it was part of Your eternal decree that Thine only-begotten Son, Jesus Christ, the Savior of the human race, should form a holy family with Mary, His blessed mother, and His foster father, Saint Joseph. In Nazareth, home life was sanctified, and a perfect example was given to every Catholic family. Grant, we beseech You, that we may fully comprehend and faithfully imitate the virtues of the Holy Family so that we may be united with them one day in their heavenly glory. Through the same Christ our Lord.

Amen

Marians of the Immaculate Conception

ASSOCIATION OF MARIAN HELPERS

STOCKBRIDGE, MA 01263

Prayers: 1-800-804-3823 • Orders: 1-800-462-7426

www.marian.org

mented on as the Gospel of the day before making his own remarks here about John Paul.

In fact, earlier in his *Angelus* message of September 16, 2007, Benedict echoes John Paul II's encyclical by speaking of how God the Father is "rich in mercy" toward all his children and calls us to do likewise:

> True religion thus consists in being attuned to [God's] Heart, "rich in mercy," which asks us to love everyone, even those who are distant and our enemies, imitating the Heavenly Father who respects the freedom of each one and draws everyone to himself with the invincible power of his faithfulness.

Third, notice the particular context in our time in which Pope Benedict speaks of John Paul "prophetically intuit[ing]" the "urgent pastoral need" for the "witness of God's mercy." It is none other than "the tragic events of September 11, 2001" — a defining moment in the new millennium that highlights the urgent need for "Christians and people of good will to believe that God's mercy is stronger than all evil."

This is a firm conviction of John Paul II and now Pope Benedict that we sorely need today in confronting the specter of terrorism in our troubled times — lest we give in to despair. In believing it, we stand on solid ground spiritually — the trustworthy mercy of God.

Remembering John Paul II's 'Testament' of Mercy

This solid ground on which we stand includes "a testament" of mercy from Blessed John Paul II that can assure us whenever we face evil in our world — as it has Pope Benedict himself. Let me explain.

It was nearly a year after the death of John Paul II on March 26, 2006, and Benedict was visiting the Roman parish of God the Merciful Father on the Fourth Sunday of Lent. He was speaking of the importance of "a personal encounter with the Crucified and Risen Christ," based on the Sunday readings, when he turned to the testament of mercy that John Paul left the Church in his last words:

> In meditating on the Lord's mercy that was revealed totally and definitively in the mystery of the Cross, the text that John Paul II had prepared for his meeting with the faithful on April 3, [Divine

Mercy Sunday] the Second Sunday of Easter, comes to my mind.

In the divine plans it was written that he would leave us precisely on the eve of that day, Saturday, April 2 — we all remember it well — and for that reason he was unable to address his words to you. I would like to address them to you now, dear brothers and sisters, "To humanity, which sometimes seems bewildered and overwhelmed by the power of evil, self-ishness and fear, the Risen Lord offers his love that pardons, reconciles and reopens hearts to hope. It is a love that converts hearts and gives peace."

The Pope, in this last text which is like a testament, then added: "How much the world needs to understand and accept Divine Mercy!" (*Regina Caeli* message, read by Archbishop Leonardo Sandri, Substitute of the Secretariat of State, to the faithful gathered in St. Peter's Square, April 3, 2005).

In this poignant remembrance of John Paul II's last words, Benedict singles out John Paul's powerful cry of the heart to the world — which includes each of us — to understand and accept Divine Mercy. These words are like a testament we can turn to whenever we are "bewildered and overwhelmed by the power of evil," as we were on September 11, 2001. He identifies what we truly *need* most of all.

When we commit ourselves to understand and accept Divine Mercy, we are no longer helpless when confronted by evil. We are empowered through Christ to face it and place a limit upon it. As Pope Benedict told the parishioners at God the Merciful Father Church in the Diocese of Rome, "To understand and accept God's merciful love: may this be your commitment, first of all in your families and then in every neighborhood milieu."

On a personal note, perhaps Pope Benedict himself was thinking back to his own need to understand and accept the gift of Divine Mercy he received on his election as Pope through the intercession of John Paul II. He had received the gift, and now he was sharing it with the Church nearly a year after John Paul's death.

Following the example of Pope Benedict, reflect for a moment on how you have understood and accepted the gift of Divine Mercy in your own life. Did it involve a special occasion or pivotal moment in your life?

For myself, I think back to the time when my son nearly died at the age of 5 after experiencing severe, uncontrollable seizures. He was in intensive care at the local hospital for a couple of days, but he pulled through and was hospitalized for more than a week. I remember dropping everything to be at my son's bedside during those days of personal anguish. He is now 22 years old with no repercussions from the seizures. That close call helped me begin to understand and accept Divine Mercy as a dad.

Yet in understanding and accepting God's mercy, why is our trust and hope in Him important? That is the topic of our next chapter.

FULFILLING THE MANDATE

As we come to better understand and accept God's mercy and then go forth as witnesses to it, we are carrying on Blessed John Paul II's legacy of Divine Mercy for the Church and the world. We are making this legacy our own. It's a rich legacy that includes the essential insight of Divine Mercy as the limit to evil in the world, the great gift of Divine Mercy Sunday, and the prophetic witness of St. Faustina. In responding, we are especially called to proclaim John Paul's great testament of mercy: "How much the world needs to understand and accept Divine Mercy!" Most importantly, we are called to understand and accept it in our own lives. In all these ways and more, we will be following in the footsteps of Pope Benedict, the successor to the Great Mercy Pope.

CHAPTER FOUR

Our Trust and Hope in God's Mercy

Why is our trust in God's mercy significant? And what exactly does it mean to trust in God?

What is the relationship between our trust and hope in God as we respond to His mercy toward us?

These are some of the questions we answer in this chapter as we continue to explore the mercy mandate of Pope Benedict.

The Importance of Our Trust in God's Mercy

First, our trust in God's mercy is vitally important. It can make all the difference in the world. Just ask St. Faustina, Blessed John Paul II, and now Pope Benedict.

Remember in our last chapter how, after visiting The Divine Mercy Shrine in Lagiewniki, Poland, Pope Benedict spoke of Divine Mercy as "a message of trust for humanity" that St. Faustina received and then John Paul II "echoed and interpreted" as "a central message for our time: Mercy as God's power, as a barrier against the evil of the world" (General Audience, May 31, 2006).

Looking at these words afresh with our present theme in mind, Pope Benedict is saying that this message of trust in Divine Mercy is for all of humanity, which means all of us. We can trust that the Lord, in His mercy, will put a limit on evil. Such trust runs the gamut from the global to the personal — for example, praying for an end to terrorism in our world and praying for an end to violence at the local high school our child or grandchild attends.

It doesn't mean our situation will necessarily change right away, but such trust can bring us great peace and become the fundamental disposition of our hearts in our relationship with the Lord. As Pope Benedict told us on Divine Mercy Sunday 2007:

> Peace is the gift that Christ left his friends (cf. Jn 14:27) as a blessing destined for all men and women and for all peoples. It is not a peace according to a "worldly" mentality, as an equilibrium of forces, but a new reality, fruit of God's love, of his mercy. It is the peace that

Jesus earned by the price of his Blood and communicates to those who trust in him.

"Jesus, I trust in you": These words summarize the faith of the Christian, which is faith in the omnipotence of God's merciful love (*Regina Caeli* message, April 15, 2007).

The Lord's peace is not of this world. Notice how the Holy Father describes this peace that the Risen Christ brings us as "a new reality, fruit of God's love, of his mercy." It comes to us by the price of Jesus' Blood, and we receive this gift of peace as we place our trust in Him. In fact, the more we trust in the Lord, the more gifts of mercy we can receive from Him — among them, His peace.

Further, our Holy Father identifies our personal trust in Jesus as the summary of our faith as Christians. By using the words, "Jesus, I trust in you," he also evokes the motto of The Divine Mercy message, which appears on every image of the Risen Christ as The Divine Mercy.

Finally, Pope Benedict uses stirring language when he speaks of our personal trust in Jesus as the summary of our faith by describing it as "faith in the omnipotence of God's merciful love."

Thus, he underscores in an eloquent way God's mercy as the *absolute* limit to evil in our lives and in the world.

What Exactly Is Trust?

What exactly does this personal trust in the Lord Jesus involve?

Pope Benedict gave us a clue when he addressed the sick at the Shrine of The Divine Mercy in Lagiewniki, Poland, on May 27, 2006. He told them:

> You who say in the silence: "Jesus, I trust in you" teach us that there is no faith more profound, no hope more alive and no love more ardent than the faith, hope and love of a person who in the midst of suffering places himself securely in God's hands.

Pope Benedict is stressing that when we personally trust in Jesus in a difficult situation such as suffering from a sickness, our trust is not passive. Rather, it is a concrete action that involves our exercise of all three of the theological virtues — faith, hope, and love.

Our faith becomes "more profound." Our hope becomes "more alive." Our love becomes "more ardent." Through this spiritual action — in faith, hope, and love — we place ourselves "securely in God's hands." We trust in Him. It is our response to His mercy.

Here, it might be helpful to quote from the Marian Press booklet *Why Mercy Sunday?*, which I coauthored with the Divine Mercy authority Fr. George W. Kosicki, CSB:

> Trust is our faith, hope, and love in action. Trust is an action that takes in all three. It combines the past focus of our faith in what Jesus did, the present "now" dimension of His love for us, and the future dimension of hope because of what He has prepared for us in heaven.
>
> Trust, then, means to believe in Jesus, to love Him, and to hope in Him. It means to be totally absorbed in Jesus as our Lord and Savior, to rely completely upon Him. We desire to have His mind and thoughts, His will, His power, His Heart, and His total trust in the Father. To sum up, when we really trust in Jesus, we can say with the Apostle Paul: "It is no longer I who live but Christ who lives in me" (Gal 2:20).

Now, why is trust in Jesus so important in understanding Divine Mercy? Because it is our response to God's great mercy. Our part is to trust in Him (Revised edition, 2004, pp. 30-31).

'The Gift of a Trustworthy Hope'

As we seek to do our part by exercising trust, there's a special connection between our trust and the theological virtue of hope that can help us understand better why we are called to trust and hope in God's mercy.

To understand this connection, let's turn to what Pope Benedict says in his second encyclical, *Spe Salvi (Saved by Hope)*. First, he speaks of the early Christians receiving "the gift of a trustworthy hope":

We see how decisively the self-understanding of the early Christians was shaped by their having received the gift of a trustworthy hope when we compare the Christian life prior to faith, or with the situations of the followers of other religions. Paul reminds the Ephesians that before their encounter with Christ they were "without hope and without God in the world" (Eph 2:12) (*Spe Salvi*, 2).

For Christians who have been baptized and are living the Christian life, it can be hard to fathom what it would mean to live "without hope and without God in the world." However, in the largely post-Christian, secular society in which we live in the West, you need only visit the local shopping mall or cinema to get a taste of what this means. It is precisely in the midst of this kind of secular environment that we are called to make alive the hope of our salvation in Christ, which is worthy of our trust.

Thus, it is "a life-changing and life-sustaining hope" — closely linked to our "Christian faith" — that constantly challenges us to trust more in the Lord (*Spe Salvi*, 10). As such, Benedict points out how this trustworthy hope draws us inexorably to God Himself and His love:

> Man's great, true hope which holds firm in spite of all disappointment can only be God — God who loved us and who continues to love us "to the end," until all "is accomplished" (cf. Jn 13:1 and 19:30). Whoever is moved by love begins to perceive what "life" really is. He begins to perceive the meaning of the

word of hope that we encountered in the Baptismal Rite: From faith I await "eternal life" — the true life which, whole and unthreatened, in all its fullness, is simply life (*Spe Salvi*, 27).

The amazing thing to note here is that our trustworthy hope has brought us full circle to the promise of eternal life in Christ, which is accomplished by God's love at the heart of the paschal mystery of our salvation. And as we have seen time and again, this love is expressed as God's mercy toward us. For example, we just saw earlier in this chapter, at Divine Mercy Sunday 2007, Pope Benedict saying that the peace of the Risen Christ is the "fruit of God's love, of his mercy."

As Pope Benedict has emphasized on different occasions, this is why John Paul II, the Great Mercy Pope, said when he dedicated The Divine Mercy Shrine in Lagiewniki, Poland, "Apart from the mercy of God there is no source of hope for mankind." It is also why Pope Benedict in his own mandate underscores that "God's mercy" is "a source of hope for every person and the whole world." We possess a hope that is worthy of our trust. It is founded on the "omnipotence of God's merciful love," as Benedict has eloquently put it.

Our Supreme Model of Trust

To inspire us in living this call, Jesus Himself is our model par excellence in His total trust in God the Father. Pope Benedict develops Jesus' example in a masterful passage in his book *Jesus of Nazareth*. The context is the second temptation of Jesus in the desert. Satan has just quoted Psalm 91 to Jesus as he tempts the Son of God to throw Himself down from the pinnacle of the temple: "'He will give His angels charge of you,' and 'On their hands they will bear you up, lest you strike your foot against a stone'" (Mt 4:6). Jesus quotes Scripture right back in response, "Again, it is written, 'You shall not tempt the Lord your God'" (Mt 4:7).

Pope Benedict writes of Jesus' response to Satan:

> Christ did not cast himself down from the pinnacle of the Temple. He did not leap into the abyss. He did not tempt God. But he did descend into the abyss of death, into the night of abandonment, and into the desolation of the defenseless. He ventured *this* leap as an act of God's love for men. And so he knew that, ultimately, when he leaped he could only fall into the kindly hands of the Father. This brings to

light the real meaning of Psalm 91, which has to do with the right to the ultimate and unlimited trust of which the Psalm speaks: If you follow the will of God, you know that in spite of all the terrible things that happen to you, you will never lose a final refuge. You know that the foundation of the world is love, so that even when no human being can or will help you, you may go on, trusting in the One who loves you (*Jesus of Nazareth*, Doubleday, 2007, pp. 37-38, emphasis in original).

In language that takes your breath away, Pope Benedict is speaking of Jesus' complete abandonment to the Father's will in embracing the Cross. He is our model of "ultimate and unlimited trust" in God.

Take a moment and reread the Holy Father's words on how Jesus trusted when he was sorely tried. Decide to place your trust in Jesus, as He placed His in the Father, when you encounter difficulties in life. Ask yourself, "What are the situations in my life in which the Lord is asking me to trust Him more?"

For me, as a dad, I need to trust that things will work out in God's time for each of my three children. My 24-year-old daughter is planning on attending art school. My 22-year-old son serves as a medic in the army. And my 20-year-old daughter is in college, pursuing a career as a dietician. Can I let go and trust in the Lord more that He will continue to care for them, even when they make mistakes?

In our next chapter, we discover that not even Judas, the betrayer of Christ, was beyond the reach of God's mercy. This insight of Pope Benedict into the mystery of evil has some startling implications for us.

FULFILLING THE MANDATE

Growing in trust in God is our foundational response to His mercy toward us. It opens our hearts to receive God's grace and mercy — especially His gift of peace — so we can then share it with others. Jesus Himself is our supreme model of trust. Our personal trust is our faith, hope, and love put into action. We are especially called to cultivate a trustworthy hope in God's mercy. Thus, we can go forth in great confidence as "witnesses of God's mercy, a source of hope for every person and for the whole world."

CHAPTER FIVE

Christ's Betrayal and God's Mercy

The betrayal of Jesus by Judas Iscariot — one of the Master's 12 Apostles — reveals that God is "rich in mercy and forgiveness."

In fact, the Catholic Church does not teach that anyone — even Judas — is condemned to hell. "Even though he went to hang himself (cf. Mt 27:5), it is not up to us to judge his gesture, substituting ourselves for the infinitely merciful and just God."

These were among the stunning statements that Pope Benedict made to the Church and the world during his General Audience in St. Peter's Square on October 18, 2006. It was his last in a series of teachings on the 12 Apostles.

What does he mean exactly, and what are the implications for us?

Only Christ Can Judge the Human Heart

It's so easy to judge others as being damned to hell, especially notorious sinners like Judas throughout history and into the present. Consider this short list: Adolph Hitler, Joseph Stalin, Slobadan Milosevic, Pol Pot, Saddam Hussein, and Osama bin Laden.

Yet we cannot read the hearts of men and women at the time of death. We must leave this to Jesus Christ, who is the Redeemer — as does Pope Benedict in the case of Judas.

"Christ is the Lord of eternal life," teaches the *Catechism of the Catholic Church*. "Full right to pass definitive judgment on the works and hearts of men belongs to Him as redeemer of the world" (679). And Christ's judgment of each human soul is not arbitrary but based on His complete knowledge of the true condition of the soul. As the *Catechism* states, "When He comes at the end of time to judge the living and the dead, the glorious Christ will reveal the secret disposition of hearts and will render to each man according to his works and according to his acceptance or refusal of grace" (682).

An important implication for us, then, is to guard our hearts against passing judgment on someone else's soul. For example, in our heart of hearts have we judged and damned to hell Saddam Hussein and Osama Bin Laden? Closer to home is there a particularly bothersome or difficult family member, friend, or co-worker whom we have judged as unworthy of heaven?

Let's repent right now of such a critical or judgmental spirit toward anyone we know. Instead, let's decide to pray for the salvation of souls.

Pray for the Grace of Repentance for Souls in Need

God is, indeed, rich in mercy, but He does not force Himself on us. Pope Benedict underscored this point in talking about Judas and his betrayal. The Holy Father said that Christ, "in his invitations [to Judas] to follow him along the way of the beatitudes," "does not force [Judas's] will or protect it from the temptations of Satan, respecting human freedom."

This is precisely where we can come in as intercessors — not as judges — in praying that souls in peril would respond to the grace of repentance. In fact, many Divine Mercy devotees pray The Divine Mercy Chaplet with such souls in mind, as they pray for "God's mercy on us and on the whole world."

In this regard, there's the inspiring story of the convicted Oklahoma City bomber Timothy

McVeigh who appeared to accept the grace of repentance as he went to his death. (The Marians of the Immaculate Conception published this story in the September/October 2001 issue of their *Friends of Mercy* newsletter.)

McVeigh was scheduled for execution in early June 2001, and to all appearances, he seemed beyond redemption. Then, in the two days before his execution, thousands of Divine Mercy devotees began to contact each other through e-mail and pray the chaplet for him. The e-mail message to pray for McVeigh reached at least 5,000 people in less than 18 hours.

The encouraging news with McVeigh is that at the last hour before his execution on June 11, 2001, he was asked if he wanted to see a priest. And McVeigh, who had seemed openly defiant to the end, agreed to see a priest and received the Sacraments. As Independent Catholic News reported from Indiana, "Fr. Ron Ashmore of St. Margaret Mary Church, said McVeigh asked to see Terre Haute prison chaplain Fr. Frank Roof in the execution chamber minutes before his death." In the news account, Fr. Ashmore said of McVeigh's decision to see a priest, "Tim was raised a Catholic. He knows when you ask for [the Sacraments], it's like saying, 'I'm sorry for everything I've done, Lord. Please love me.'"

That was in 2001. What about us today? Can we find it in our hearts to pray for the grace of repentance for al-Qaeda terrorists who plot the murder of innocents? Can we pick up our beads and pray The Divine Mercy Chaplet today with this intention in mind?

Our Main Adversary Is Satan

When Pope Benedict considers the motives for Judas's betrayal of Jesus, he makes clear that Satan is the main adversary working through Judas. Yes, the Holy Father notes, there's Judas's "greed for money" and the fact that "Jesus did not fit into his program for the political-militaristic liberation of his own nation."

But Benedict goes on to say that "the Gospel texts insist on another aspect." The Pope cites John the Evangelist that "the devil had already put it into the heart of Judas Iscariot, Simon's son, to betray him" (Jn 13:2) and Luke when he writes, "Then Satan entered into Judas called Iscariot, who was of the number of the twelve" (Lk 22:3).

Pope Benedict concludes: "In this way, one moves beyond historical motivations and explanations based on the personal responsibility of Judas, who shamefully ceded to a temptation of the Evil One."

Here, it is helpful to remember the words of St. Paul: "For our struggle is not with flesh and blood but with the principalities, with the powers, with the world rulers of this present darkness, with the evil spirits in the heavens" (Eph 6:12). With all this in mind, we need to realize that we are engaged in spiritual warfare against Satan when we see evil at work in our lives, in the lives of others, and in our world.

Jesus has the victory and is, indeed, seated at God's right hand in glory. Here on earth, though, Satan seeks to oppose Him at every turn and tempts human beings to join him.

As you and I face daily spiritual warfare in this life, I strongly recommend the Prayer to St. Michael the Archangel during times of temptation throughout our day. Saint Michael is the great warrior angel who cast Satan and his followers out of heaven after they rebelled against God; the great Pope Leo XIII composed this prayer to St. Michael after a vision:

> Saint Michael the Archangel, defend us in battle. Be our defense against the

wickedness and snares of the devil. May God rebuke him we humbly pray. And do you, O prince of the heavenly host, by the power of God, cast into hell Satan and all the evil spirits who prowl about the world seeking the ruin of souls. Amen.

Here, in Our Lady of Mercy Oratory at the Marian Helpers Center in Stockbridge, Massachusetts, we recite this prayer at the end of daily Mass. My wife and I also pray it at the end of our nightly walks before bedtime.

As we pray to St. Michael, we can remember especially souls whom we think are under spiritual attack.

The Transforming Power of Love and Mercy

At the end of his General Audience, Pope Benedict encourages us to "never despair of God's mercy," because the love and mercy of God will always win out in the end.

Interestingly, the Holy Father points out how the betrayal of Christ by Judas is a supreme example of this unfailing, providential love of God because it led to our salvation:

When we think of the negative role Judas played, we must consider it according to the lofty ways in which God leads events. His betrayal led to the death of Jesus, who transformed this tremendous torment into a space of salvific love by consigning himself to the Father (cf. Gal 2:20; Eph 5:2, 25).

The word "to betray" is the version of a Greek word that means "to consign." Sometimes the subject is even God in person; it was he who for love "consigned" Jesus for all of us (Rom 8:32). In his mysterious salvific plan, God assumes Judas's inexcusable gesture as the occasion for the total gift of his Son for the redemption of the world.

Read these words over, letting your mind soak up their meaning. Pope Benedict is saying that Judas, in a mysterious way, advanced God's ultimate purpose, which was and is to save us from our sins. Thus, God in Christ thwarted the evil designs of Satan and of Judas in achieving precisely the good of our salvation!

Inspired by this triumph of God's mercy over evil, let's decide anew to place our complete trust in Jesus, our Redeemer. Let's marvel in how Divine Mercy is revealed in Jesus' betrayal by

Judas. May we "never despair of God's mercy," even in the face of the great evils of our own time — abortion, terrorism and war, the breakdown of the family. There is no evil that the transforming, redeeming power of God's love and mercy cannot overcome.

Through our prayers and sacrifices joined to those of Jesus on the Cross, let's strive to make a total gift of ourselves for the redemption of the world. Then let's wait patiently, but with confidence, for God in His mercy to act.

Benedict, Our Mercy Pope

As we wait with patience for God's mercy to fall, let's consider *why* these statements are significant for Pope Benedict and his teaching on Divine Mercy. First, consider that Benedict is offering fresh insights into God's mercy and the mystery of evil without mentioning John Paul II.

Second, he is speaking a year and a half after the passing of John Paul, and it isn't on a special occasion associated with Divine Mercy or John Paul. Instead, his remarks come at his weekly General Audience in which he is just completing a series on the 12 Apostles.

The conclusion is unmistakable: Benedict

has integrated John Paul II's key understanding of Divine Mercy as the ultimate limit to evil into his own teaching. In that light, he is offering new insights into the mystery of evil as our Mercy Pope. We would do well to take note and listen.

In fact, in our next chapter, Pope Benedict looks at the parable of the Good Samaritan with fresh insight that can transform how we serve our neighbor in need. You might even call his insight electrifying.

FULFILLING THE MANDATE

God's mercy is intended for all sinners. We should guard our hearts against judging the souls of others, including notorious sinners like Judas. God alone is qualified to sit in judgment over human hearts. Instead, we should pray that sinners will turn back to the Lord and receive the grace of repentance. Further, in our battle against evil, we should be mindful that Satan, not human beings, is our main adversary. Therefore, we should engage in spiritual warfare for the salvation of souls.

In our struggles, we can be comforted to know that what Satan intended for our harm can ultimately be transformed into something good and salvific through God's mercy. The supreme example of this is the transforming power of Christ's Cross in the face of Judas's betrayal and Satan's diabolical purposes. Never despairing of God's mercy, we know that our own prayers and sacrifices joined to the Cross of Christ can make a difference in overcoming evil. These astounding insights into the mystery of evil demonstrate that Benedict is our Mercy Pope, who is guiding us in our witness to God's unfathomable mercy for all souls.

Chapter Six

'The Lightning Flash of Mercy'

It was Friday evening, August 3, 2007. It had been a stressful work week for me — on deadline for *Marian Helper* magazine, which I edit for the Marians of the Immaculate Conception. So I decided to treat myself by picking up a copy of *The New York Times*.

Well, imagine my surprise when I saw mercy writ large in the day's headlines, right on the front page.

Let me explain. *The Times* was reporting on the collapse of the Interstate 35W bridge in Minneapolis on August 1, which had stunned the nation and raised serious concerns about the safety of our nation's infrastructure of highways and bridges. Of course, the immediate concern in the aftermath was about the five confirmed deaths and the 20 to 30 people who remained missing after the collapse of the bridge. My initial reaction was one of great sadness and concern for the victims and their families, as well as concern for the safety of our nation's bridges.

Then, as I scanned the page, I noticed the feature with the headline: "Stunned Victim Turns Hero in Busful of Children." There was a photo alongside the story of a man named Jeremy Hernandez.

A Good Samaritan in the Day's Headlines

As I started to read the story of this Good Samaritan's act of heroism, my mood changed to joy. I couldn't help but think of Pope Benedict's book *Jesus of Nazareth* and his insight on the parable of the Good Samaritan.

But I'm getting ahead of myself. First, let me share the essentials of Ellen Barry's feature story in *The Times* about Mr. Hernandez. Then I'll get back to Pope Benedict's insight:

> By the time they reached the Interstate 35W bridge, the children on the bus were waterlogged and serene, some still in their bathing suits, ready to go home. It was a rare moment of quiet, and as the bus crossed over the Mississippi River a few of the counselors, barely out of adolescence themselves, had dropped off to sleep in their seats.
>
> What happened next is difficult to

describe, even a day later. Angi Haney, a counselor, realized first that she was not in her seat, and then that she was not touching any part of the bus, and then that "we were all just flying in the air." T.J. Mattson, a 12-year-old with wire-rimmed glasses, looked out a window and saw water on the other side. Dust filled the bus, blotting out its passengers.

And then they came to rest. Jeremy Hernandez, the whip-thin 20-year-old who worked as the summer program's gym coordinator, remembers time seemed to congeal. Then something broke the spell, and his heart began pounding, and he jumped over two rows of seats and kicked open the back door. He remembers coolers flying, and he remembers passing along children to strangers lined up like a bucket brigade.

"I just acted," Mr. Hernandez said [the day after]. "I just moved. My feet were just moving. My body was following."

The people gathered at the Waite House, the center in the Phillips neighborhood that sponsored the bus trip, were shocked, but their shock was mixed with joy. Of the 61 children and others on the school bus who plunged along with the bridge, only 14 required hospitalization, and 10 of those were quickly released. None died.

Notice how this Good Samaritan simply acted to save lives at that chaotic moment aboard the bus. He didn't stop and analyze the situation.

'The Lightning Flash of Mercy'

Keep that in mind as we turn to Pope Benedict's insight on Jesus' parable of the Good Samarian in the Gospel of Luke (see 10:25-37).

A man has just been robbed and beaten, and he is lying by the side of the road. A priest and a Levite pass by on the other side of the road. Will anyone stop to help?

Benedict picks up the narrative here, writing:

And now the Samaritan enters the stage. What will he do? [Unlike the expert in the Law who had just been questioning Jesus] he does not ask how far his obligations of solidarity extend. Nor does he ask about the merits required for eternal life. Something else happens: His heart is wrenched open. The Gospel uses the word that in Hebrew had originally referred to the mother's womb and maternal care. Seeing this man in such a state is a blow that strikes him "viscerally," touching his soul. "He had compassion" — that is how we translate the text today, diminishing its original vitality. Struck in his soul by the lightning flash of mercy, he himself now becomes a neighbor, heedless of any question or danger. The burden of the question thus shifts here. The issue is no longer which other person is a neighbor to me or not. The question is about me. I have to become the neighbor, and when I do, the other person counts for me "as myself" (*Jesus of Nazareth*, Doubleday, 2007, p. 197).

In this light, can't we say that Jeremy Hernandez was "struck in his soul by the lightning flash of mercy" when "time seemed to congeal" and he knew what he had to do? Just as the Samaritan stopped by the side of the road to aid the seriously injured man who had been robbed and beaten, so Mr. Hernandez "jumped over two rows of seats" on the bus and "kicked open the back door" to save the lives of his fellow passengers. The same merciful response led him to pass along "children [from the bus] to strangers lined up like a bucket brigade."

Along with this dramatic rescue, one powerful image of this lightning flash of mercy that never ceases to amaze me is how firefighters risk life and limb in the face of roaring flames to save people trapped in fires. They are the epitome of the Good Samaritan as the one who "now becomes a neighbor, heedless of any question or danger."

But you and I face less dramatic examples of this call to serve our neighbor in need. Last year, in my parish of Sacred Heart in Pittsfield, Massachusetts, we took up a second collection for a family in desperate straits. Along with my fellow parishioners, I was immediately moved to be as generous as possible. The mother had just suffered a severe heart attack, while the father had recently lost his job. To make matters worse, it was a family with small children.

Yet how many times have I failed miserably to respond to the lightning flash of mercy? I sense a prompting to stop and help a homeless person on the street, but I squelch the urge and pass by on the other side of the road. It's Saturday, and I feel a pang of conscience about not helping my elderly neighbor down the street by offering to pick up her medications and buy her groceries. I rationalize that I'm too busy with my own chores at home.

What about you? Have you ever been struck in your soul "by the lightning flash of mercy"? Think of the times when you have responded or failed to respond.

'A Heart Which Sees'

Interestingly, in his first encyclical, *Deus Caritas Est (God Is Love)*, Pope Benedict also touches on the parable of the Good Samaritan in his section on the distinctiveness of the Church's charitable activity:

> Following the example given in the parable of the Good Samaritan, Christian charity is first of all the simple response to immediate needs and specific situations: feeding the hungry, clothing the naked, caring for and healing the sick, visiting those in prison, etc. ...

> One does not make the world more human by refusing to act humanely here and now. We contribute to a better world

95

only by personally doing good now, with full commitment and whenever we have the opportunity, independently of partisan strategies and programs. The Christian's program — the program of the Good Samaritan, the program of Jesus — is "a heart which sees." This heart sees where love is needed and acts accordingly (31).

In the first paragraph of this excerpt, Benedict speaks in a similar vein about his teaching on the parable of the Good Samaritan in his book *Jesus of Nazareth*. We are called to respond to "immediate needs and specific situations" in caring for our neighbor. Then he begins to enumerate the corporal works of mercy, which provide a number of situations in which we are called to help our neighbor in need.

The Pope's remarks evoke the Last Judgment discourse in Matthew, where Jesus says that we will be judged on our performing the corporal works of mercy for those in need out of love for Him. In summing up, Jesus, in the person of the King, tells the righteous: "Amen, I say to you, what you did for one of these least brothers of Mine, you did for Me"(Mt 25:40).

In the second paragraph of the excerpt, the Pope describes "the program of the Good Samaritan" as "a heart which sees" "where love is needed and acts accordingly." Here, we can think of those in the Last Judgment discourse of Matthew who are condemned precisely because they did not perform works of mercy when they saw their brother or sister in need (see Mt 25:41-46). Even more specifically, we can think of the parable of the Rich Man and Lazarus where the Rich Man failed to notice Lazarus, a poor man covered with sores, who was lying right at his door (see Lk 16:19-31).

Do we have eyes to see those who are in need in our neighborhoods, parishes, and places of work? Or are we literally passing them by on our way home?

I'll never forget a couple of years ago when I got a flat tire on my way home from work. I had pulled off to the side of the road and was just getting ready to change the tire while dressed in a sports coat, tie, and slacks. Noticing me fumble with the car jack in my nice clothes, a couple of workmen in a pick-up truck pulled over and offered to change my tire. They had hearts that saw me in my need.

A Foundation for Our Service to Others

How can we best develop a heart that sees? For Pope Benedict, the key is an intimacy with the Lord that nurtures the giving of ourselves in service and a "radical humility" like that of Christ Himself upon the Cross:

> Practical activity will always be insufficient, unless it visibly expresses a love for man, a love nourished by an encounter with Christ. My deep personal sharing in the needs and sufferings of others becomes a sharing of my very self with them: If my gift is not to prove a source of humiliation, I must give to others not only something that is my own, but my very self; I must be personally present in my gift.

> This proper way of serving others also leads to humility. The one who serves does not consider himself superior to the one served, however miserable his situation at the moment may be. Christ took the lowest place in the world — the Cross — and by this radical humility he redeemed us and constantly comes to our

aid. Those who are in a position to help others will realize that in doing so they themselves receive help; being able to help others is no merit or achievement of their own. This duty is a grace. The more we do for others, the more we understand and can appropriate the words of Christ: "We are useless servants" (Lk 17:10). We recognize that we are not acting on the basis of any superiority or greater personal efficiency, but because the Lord has graciously enabled us to do so (*Deus Caritas Est,* 34-35).

We develop such intimacy with the Lord through daily prayer, reflection on the Scriptures, and frequent reception of the Sacraments. Above all, intimacy with our Savior is fostered by receiving Him regularly in Holy Communion and being quick to confess any serious sins in the Sacrament of Reconciliation. Out of such a prayerful and sacramental life, we are empowered to give our lives in service to others and to do it with real humility, as servants of our Lord and Master, Jesus Christ.

The Pope is concerned that without this kind of foundation, we will be prone to take a secular approach to our charitable service. Yet then what will we do without the love and mercy of God to sustain us — when we reach the end of our own human resources? In that vein, he writes:

It is time to reaffirm the importance of prayer in the face of activism and the growing secularism of many Christians engaged in charitable work. Clearly, the Christian who prays does not claim to be able to change God's plans or correct what he has foreseen. Rather, he seeks an encounter with the Father of Jesus Christ, asking God to be present with the consolation of the Spirit to him and his work. A personal relationship with God and an abandonment to his will can prevent man from being demeaned and save him from falling prey to the teaching of fanaticism and terrorism. An authentically religious attitude prevents man from presuming to judge God, accusing him of allowing poverty and failing to have compassion for his creatures. When people claim to build a case against God in defense of man, on whom can they depend when human activity proves powerless? (*Deus Caritas Est,* 37).

Speaking for myself, I know that in all my service and work for others, personal prayer and daily Mass are my lifeline. Especially when I miss daily Mass, I find that my strength and concentration start to flag.

What about you? What is the spiritual foundation for your life of service? Take a minute or two to examine your own spiritual life.

Moving on, in our next chapter, we discover that Pope Benedict has especially called on the sick and youth to be witnesses of God's mercy. Why has he singled them out?

FULFILLING THE MANDATE

As God has shown mercy to us, we are called to show mercy to others, especially those in greatest need. Otherwise, our witness to God's mercy will lack credibility and integrity. Like the heart of the Good Samaritan, our hearts should be disposed to serving our neighbor. To use Pope Benedict's powerful image, we never know when we may be struck in our souls "by the lightning flash of mercy" upon encountering someone in great need. Or to use another of Benedict's images, we need "a heart which sees" "where love is needed and acts accordingly."

Such a disposition of the heart is best fostered by a prayerful and sacramental life, so we are not running on empty when we are called to serve others in challenging situations that stretch us. In this regard, our love of neighbor should flow from our love of God, the One who first loved us. Then we will be empowered to give of ourselves in service and to do it humbly, as Jesus our Master did upon the Cross.

CHAPTER SEVEN

Special Witnesses of God's Mercy

The sick remind us of the mystery of suffering in our broken world, while our youth point to the promise of a vibrant future. What do these two groups have in common?

In a phrase: a witness of mercy to the world.

For Pope Benedict, both the sick and the youth are called to be special witnesses of God's mercy. He calls the sick in their suffering "the most eloquent witnesses of God's mercy." With today's youth, he speaks of passing on to them the "Flame of Mercy," so "they might be heralds of Love and Divine Mercy in the world."

'The Most Eloquent Witnesses of God's Mercy'

Let's turn first to the witness of the sick.

When Pope Benedict visited the Shrine of The Divine Mercy in Lagiewniki, Poland, on May 27, 2006, he addressed the sick with these

© Marie Romagnano

On May 27, 2006, Pope Benedict XVI addresses the sick and their caregivers at the International Shrine of The Divine Mercy in Lagiewniki, Poland: There, the Pontiff referred to the sick as "the most eloquent witnesses of God's mercy."

poignant words:

> On this occasion we encounter two mysteries: the mystery of human suffering and the mystery of Divine Mercy. At first sight these two mysteries seem to be opposed to one another. But when we study them more deeply in the light of faith, we find that they are placed in reciprocal harmony through the mystery of the Cross of Christ. As Pope John Paul II said in this place: "The Cross is the most profound bowing down of the Divinity towards man ... the Cross is like a touch of eternal love on the most painful wounds of humanity's earthly existence" (August 17, 2002). Dear friends who are sick, who are marked by suffering in body or soul, you are most closely united to the Cross of Christ, and at the same time, you are the most eloquent witnesses of God's mercy. Through you and through your suffering, he bows down toward humanity with love. You who say in silence: "Jesus, I trust in you" teach us that there is no faith more profound, no hope more alive

and no love more ardent than the faith, hope and love of a person who in the midst of suffering places himself securely in God's hands.

Notice how, in beautiful imagery inspired by John Paul II's own visit to Lagiewniki, Pope Benedict speaks of Christ "bow[ing] down toward humanity with love." This gesture of love from the Lord comes in response to the sick and their suffering, which is united to His own on the Cross. The credibility of their profound and silent witness stems from their deep, abiding trust in the Lord Jesus precisely in the midst of their suffering and pain. Their faith becomes more profound, their hope more alive, and their love more ardent through their trust in the crucified One. They present an ever-fresh and compelling witness to the Cross of Christ.

In this regard, we might even wonder if John Paul II — who was himself in his final years when he visited Lagiewniki in 2002 — was in the back of Pope Benedict's mind when he speaks here of the sick as "the most eloquent witnesses of God's mercy." Benedict certainly remembered how Pope John Paul II suffered from the debilitating effects of Parkinson's disease in his last years, as he visibly struggled to speak and had to use a cane or be transported on a platform in order to get around. Especially in the closing weeks of his life, John Paul was rendered almost completely silent in his suffering. Who can forget, for example, how he was unable to speak and could only bless the crowd in St. Peter's Square on his last Easter Sunday?

Christ Accompanies the Sick

Interestingly, Pope Benedict also spoke of the sick and God's mercy on his visit to Lourdes, France, in September 2008 to mark the 150th anniversary year of the apparitions of the Blessed Virgin Mary to St. Bernadette. Here, he underscored how the sick are not alone in their witness of suffering but are accompanied by "Christ the healer" and Mary, who comes to them as a merciful mother.

In His mercy, Christ comes in a special way to strengthen the infirm through the Sacrament of the Anointing of the Sick, as Benedict stressed in his homily at Lourdes on September 15, 2008:

> Christ imparts his salvation by means of the sacraments, and especially in the case of those suffering from sickness or

disability, by means of the grace of the sacrament of the sick. ... Here and now ... it is possible to entrust oneself to God's mercy, as manifested through the grace of the sacrament of the sick. Bernadette herself, in the course of a life that was often marked by sickness, received this sacrament four times. The grace of this sacrament consists in welcoming Christ the healer into ourselves. However, Christ is not a healer in the manner of the world. In order to heal us, he does not remain outside the suffering that is experienced; he eases it by coming to dwell within the one stricken by illness, to bear it and live it with him. Christ's presence comes to break the isolation which pain induces. Man no longer bears the burden alone: As a suffering member of Christ, he is conformed to Christ in his self-offering to the Father, and he participates, in him, in the coming to birth of the new creation.

The sick, then, are not alone in their witness of suffering. No, through the Sacrament of the Anointing of the Sick, Christ Himself comes inside each one who is ill to help him bear it and even to live the suffering with him. Christ the healer gives the sick person the grace to trust in His mercy, which makes this union in suffering possible. Further, as the sick are conformed to the Lord Jesus in His sacrifice to the Father, they share in bringing forth the new creation in Christ, making their witness truly enduring and eloquent.

God also gives the sick a special gift of His mercy in the Blessed Virgin Mary. As a spiritual mother, she comes to us, her children, in our need, Pope Benedict said in his homily at Lourdes on Sept. 14, 2008:

> Dear Brothers and Sisters, the primary purpose of the shrine at Lourdes is to be a place of encounter with God in prayer and a place of service to our brothers and sisters, notably through the welcome given to the sick, the poor and all who suffer. In this place, Mary comes to us as a mother, always open to the needs of her children. Through the light which streams from her face, God's mercy is made manifest. Let us allow ourselves to be touched by her gaze, which tells us that we are all loved by God and never abandoned by him!

So, along with the sacramental presence of Jesus Himself, Mary as a mother accompanies the sick in their suffering. Indeed, her maternal love toward the sick makes the mercy of God manifest in our midst.

But there's even more here. Earlier in this homily, Benedict had reminded the faithful at Lourdes that Mary revealed her name to Bernadette when she told the peasant girl: "I am the Immaculate Conception." And since she was conceived without sin, surely Mary Immaculate is herself the greatest recipient of Divine Mercy. As such, no human being is better equipped than Mary Immaculate herself to manifest God's mercy, especially to the sick in their great need. Indeed, her presence alongside the sick reminds them "that we are all loved by God and never abandoned by him."

Our Suffering Can Be Redemptive

Consider what all this means to each of us in our witness to God's mercy when we are sick — or anytime we suffer for whatever reason. Pope Benedict has given us a way to make our witness eloquent.

Here's how. Whenever we are sick, you and I are called not to waste our suffering but to join it to that of Christ and place our trust in Him. Further, whenever we receive the Sacrament of the Anointing of the Sick, Christ accompanies us in a special way, actually coming inside to help us bear the burden of our suffering. With a mother's love, Mary, too, helps us in our struggles. We can readily confide in her, since she understands God's mercy best as the Immaculate Conception.

Such a witness is easier said than done. I recall when in November 1998, I had emergency surgery to remove my gall bladder, which was seriously infected due to impacted gall stones. After coming home from the hospital, my recovery was further complicated when I came down with strep throat. As a result, I had to spend a couple of weeks in considerable pain.

All I could do was lie in bed and largely suffer in silence, knowing that I was missing deadlines at work and wondering how things were going with a major Divine Mercy event that I was helping to organize for my parish. At some point, I remember entrusting it all into God's hands and asking Mary for her help. I believe that this trust in the Lord enabled me to try, even if fitfully, to offer my sufferings for my co-workers at work and for those assisting on the parish project.

Now, looking back, I see that the work got done at the office and the event went well in my parish. God was in charge not me, and He gave me the blessed opportunity to witness to Him through my suffering, instead of doing the work myself.

What about you? Recall a time when you were sick and called to be a witness of God's mercy.

There's also another important point to make here. Along with approaching our own sickness with trust, we are called to encourage the sick in our midst to be witnesses to God's mercy. It might involve a phone call or a visit to a home-bound senior in our neighborhood or to a family member who is in the hospital for surgery. Whatever the situation, we can share with them about Pope Benedict's teaching, so they don't waste the precious gift of their suffering.

Sharing this perspective with the sick can be helpful, because our post-Christian society has largely lost sight of the redemptive value of suffering and, therefore, of how it can be an eloquent witness of Christ's presence among us.

'Heralds of Love and Divine Mercy'

Let's turn now to how Pope Benedict has called the youth of the world to be witnesses to God's mercy.

During his pastoral visit to Poland, the Holy

Father met with an estimated 500,000 young people at Blonie Park in Krakow on May 27, 2006. He emphasized building on the Rock of Christ the Lord and told the youth of Christ's personal love for them. Significantly, he spoke before a gigantic Divine Mercy image and said, after his return to Rome, that he had "symbolically consigned the 'Flame of Mercy' to the crowds of young people who had come, so that they might be heralds of Love and Divine Mercy in the world" (General Audience, May 31).

"To build on Christ and with Christ means to build on a foundation that is called 'crucified love,'" the Holy Father told the youth at Blonie Park. "It means to build with Someone who, ... from the Cross, extends his arms and repeats for all eternity: 'O man, I give my life for you because I love you.'"

Here, Benedict uses stirring words to draw the youth of Poland to the heart of the paschal mystery, Christ's love and mercy for each of us on the Cross — His "crucified love."

Even before Pope Benedict spoke these powerful words to youth in Poland, he was mentioning God's mercy to youth in his own homeland of Germany. The opportunity came at World Youth Day in Cologne, Germany, August 16-21, 2005, with the theme: "We have come to worship him" (Mt 2:2). It was his first pastoral visit as Pope outside Italy, and the event drew an estimated 1.2 million youth.

In developing the theme of all the nations like the Magi coming to worship Christ, Pope Benedict told the young people in his welcoming remarks:

> To all of you I appeal: Open wide your hearts to God! Let yourselves be surprised by Christ! Let him have "the right of free speech" during these days!
>
> Open the doors of your freedom to his merciful love! Share your joys and pains with Christ, and let him enlighten your minds with his light and touch your hearts with his grace.
>
> In these days blessed with sharing and joy, may you have a liberating experience of the Church as the place where God's merciful love reaches out to all people. In the Church and through the Church you will meet Christ, who is waiting for you (Cologne-Poller Wiesen, August 18, 2005).

Benedict's tone here is exuberant, and he invites the youth from throughout the world to open their hearts and give Christ the freedom to share His merciful love with them. On their World Youth Day journey with the Magi, he also stresses the Church "as the place where God's merciful love reaches out to all people." The goal is a personal encounter with Christ, not in isolation, but in and through the Church.

The Holy Father is mindful as well that the Church in 2005 was celebrating a Year of the Eucharist. So, he further invites the youth in his welcoming remarks to see in the awe that filled the Magi upon encountering the Savior, a call to likewise approach Christ with awe in the Holy Eucharist. And tellingly, he speaks of the Eucharistic Christ present in the "Tabernacle of Mercy":

> "The Magi are filled with awe by what they see: heaven on earth and earth in heaven; man in God and God in man; they see enclosed in a tiny body the One whom the entire world cannot contain" (St. Peter Chrysologus, Serm. 160, n. 2).

> In these days, during this "Year of the Eucharist," we will turn with the same awe to Christ present in the Tabernacle of Mercy, in the Sacrament of the Altar.

Here, the Holy Father is leading the youth to Christ in the Eucharist and teaching them to do so with an attitude of reverence for the Divine Majesty, who was present at Bethlehem and is now present in our tabernacles. Further, just as he did with the Sacrament of the Anointing of the Sick, he is framing the Sacrament in terms of God's mercy.

During his address at the youth vigil for World Youth Day, Pope Benedict picks up the thread of mercy again. This time, he is speaking of how the Magi are changed men after their encounter with Jesus, the true King:

> [The Magi] must become men of truth, of justice, of goodness, of forgiveness, of mercy. They will no longer ask: How can this serve me? Instead, they will have to ask: How can I serve God's presence in the world? They must learn to lose their life and in this way to find it. Having left Jerusalem behind, they must not deviate from the path marked out by the true King, as they follow Jesus (Cologne-Marienfeld, August 20, 2005).

With reference to mercy, the Holy Father is saying that as the Magi have received mercy through their encounter with the newborn King, now they are called to become men of forgiveness and mercy themselves.

Later, in his address, the Pope encouraged the youth in Cologne to do likewise — following the Magi and "the great multitude of the saints."

What are the implications for today's youth? Through a life-changing encounter with Christ, especially in the Eucharist, they are called to go forth as young men and women of forgiveness and mercy — or as Pope Benedict put it in Poland — "heralds of Love and Divine Mercy in the world."

The Girl Scouts Respond to the Call

As I finish writing this book, I can share an exciting example of Girl Scouts in our own country spreading the Good News of God's mercy. Although I doubt any of them were present in Poland or Germany when the Pope spoke, they're responding to the same call as part of The Divine Mercy movement in the Church.

Here's an excerpt from an online story that will fill in the picture:

From its very beginnings nearly 100 years ago, the motivating force in Girl

Scouting has been a spiritual life. Girl Scouts promise to serve God and country and "to help people at all times."

With that in mind, it was probably only a matter of time before Girl Scouts discovered the message of Divine Mercy as revealed to St. Maria Faustina in the 1930s, a call for spiritual renewal through trust in God and love of neighbor.

[In autumn 2008], a Girl Scout Troop in Texas pinned and sewed the portraiture of Jesus, The Divine Mercy, on their sashes and vests, earning scouting's first-ever Divine Mercy Award. Alongside other awards, which give recognition for proficiency in such areas as health, sports, technology, and the environment, the Divine Mercy Award distinguishes Troop 810 in San Antonio as young women who vow to continue St. Faustina's mission of spreading Divine Mercy. "Learning about St. Faustina has inspired me to now pray the Chaplet of The Divine Mercy each night and to pray for the whole world's sins rather than just my own or my immediate family's," says Nina

Eng, a ninth grader. "It has helped me become more thoughtful for the world."

Members of Troop 810 not only completed the requirements for the award, they also wrote the book on it — literally. Through the Archdiocese of San Antonio and with assistance from many others and after four months of serious dedication and personal and spiritual growth, Troop 810 has put together a 44-page Divine Mercy Award book. The book serves as both a workbook for scouts seeking to earn the award and a primer for The Divine Mercy message and devotion. It includes requirements for the award; suggestions for living the message of Divine Mercy; instructions for praying the Chaplet of The Divine Mercy; art projects; and many other interesting topics pertaining to The Divine Mercy.

"We hope we can reach so many more Girl Scouts and Boy Scouts and inspire them to give greater glory to God and help St. Faustina spread the message and devotion of The Divine Mercy," says

Troop 810 Leader Mary Ellen Madalinski (Felix Carroll, www.thedivinemercy.org, November 7, 2008).

Please join me in praying for the success of this initiative among the Girl Scouts. As you do, consider ways that you can encourage youth in your family, neighborhood, and parish to be "heralds of Love and Divine Mercy in the world."

Perhaps your parish has a youth group that would be interested in learning more about Divine Mercy. How might you help facilitate that? Or if you have young people at home, how could you encourage them to receive God's mercy and live mercifully? Remember Pope Benedict's advice that it all starts with a life-changing, personal encounter with Jesus Himself, especially in the Eucharist.

Turning to our next chapter, we'll explore Pope Benedict's involvement in the first World Apostolic Congress on Mercy in Rome in April 2008. We will discover *why* his involvement was crucial and how it laid the groundwork for his mandate.

FULFILLING THE MANDATE

Pope Benedict calls the sick to be "the most eloquent witnesses of God's mercy." Whenever we are sick or suffer for any reason, we are called to trust in God's mercy and join our sufferings to those of Christ on the Cross. We should encourage the sick in our midst to do likewise. Further, Christ accompanies us in our suffering, especially through the Sacrament of the Anointing of the Sick. As our spiritual mother, Mary also manifests God's mercy toward us, particularly when we are sick. In a world that doesn't understand the value of redemptive suffering, the eloquent witness of the sick is urgently needed. Pope John Paul II gave the world a most eloquent witness of God's mercy through his suffering in his final years.

In the case of our youth, Pope Benedict encourages them to be "heralds of Love and Divine Mercy in the world." The Pope even speaks of passing on to them the "Flame of Mercy." He invites them to a personal encounter with Christ in and through the Church — especially by approaching the Eucharistic Lord in the "Tabernacle of Mercy." As they receive mercy from Christ, they are called to go forth into the world as young men and women of mercy and forgiveness. We should encourage our young people to embrace this call.

CHAPTER EIGHT

Benedict and the World Mercy Congress

The first World Apostolic Congress on Mercy (WACOM), held in Rome on April 2-6, 2008, definitely bears the stamp of Pope Benedict. As we shall see, he blessed and encouraged this important initiative in the life of the Church, which was inspired by John Paul II's Divine Mercy legacy. In key remarks only days before the Congress, he set the table for this celebration of God's mercy. Most importantly, at the open and close of the World Mercy Congress, Benedict was front and center: opening it with Holy Mass for the Great Mercy Pope, John Paul II, and delivering his mandate at its conclusion.

Let's take each point, and as we do, we'll unpack the significance of the first World Mercy Congress.

The Congress and Benedict's Blessing

First, let's provide some background on World Apostolic Congresses in the life of the

Felix Carroll

On April 2, 2008, Pope Benedict XVI opens the first World Apostolic Congress on Mercy in St. Peter's Square with Holy Mass on the third anniversary of the death of John Paul II, the Great Mercy Pope: In his homily, the Holy Father singled out the nearly 4,000 delegates present for the Congress, highlighting how they would "deepen [John Paul II's] rich Magisterium on the subject" of God's mercy.

Benedict and the Congress

Church, then cover the genesis of the first World Apostolic Congress on Mercy, and finally turn to Pope Benedict's encouragement of this new apostolic endeavor.

At Apostolic Congresses, the faithful gather from around the world in a prominent city to celebrate a particular mystery of the faith. Such Congresses have the backing of the Vatican and are celebrations of the universal Church.

International Eucharistic Congresses started in the 19th century, then Marian Congresses at the beginning of the 20th century. Now, the first World Mercy Congress was held in 2008, at the beginning of the 21st century.

These Congresses typically involve talks, prayer, time for Eucharistic Adoration, and celebration of the Sacraments to help the faithful deepen their understanding of the particular mystery of the faith and live it — be it the Holy Eucharist, the Blessed Virgin Mary, or God's mercy. Further, such Congresses are held every several years. For example, the next World Congress on Mercy is slated for October 2011 in Krakow, Poland.

But we're getting ahead of ourselves. The idea of a World Mercy Congress came in July 2005 at the end of an international retreat for priests and their pastoral co-workers, which took place at the International Shrine of The Divine Mercy in Lagiewniki, Poland. Led by Cardinals Christoph Schönborn of Vienna, Austria, and Philippe Barbarin of Lyons, France, more than 500 clergy, religious, and laity devoted to God's mercy gathered for the retreat from around the world.

There in Lagiewniki, it was Pope John Paul II's entrustment of the world to Divine Mercy and his consecration of the International Shrine in 2002 that inspired the retreatants to develop the idea for a World Mercy Congress. The goal was to fulfill John Paul's mission of mercy when he said right before his solemn act of entrustment: "From here there must go forth 'the spark which will prepare the world for [Jesus'] final coming' (*Diary of St. Faustina*, 1732). This spark needs to be lighted by the grace of God. This fire of mercy needs to be passed on to the world." So the World Congress was seen at its inception as an important means for spreading "this fire of mercy" on the earth to reach all souls.

Thus, it was that in February 2006, Cardinal Schönborn presented the idea to Pope Benedict and "received his encouragement and blessing," according to WACOM's official website www.worldapostoliccongressonmercy.org. And this comes as no surprise since, as we saw in chapter three, Benedict has embraced John Paul II's legacy of Divine Mercy and made it his own. Further, it was no accident that Benedict approved opening the Congress on April 2, 2008, the third anniversary of the death of John Paul II, and holding it in Rome at the heart of the Church.

Setting the Table for the Congress

Now, we can turn to how Pope Benedict set the table for the Congress.

First, it's fascinating that in September 2007 — only seven months before the World Mercy Congress — Benedict made this remarkable statement about John Paul II, whom he knew was the inspiration behind the Congress: "In our time, humanity needs a strong proclamation and witness of God's mercy. Beloved John Paul II, a great apostle of Divine Mercy, prophetically intuited this urgent pastoral need" (*Angelus* message, September 16, 2007).

We've studied these words before in light of Benedict's appreciation for John Paul's legacy of Divine Mercy. But let's take a second look with a focus on how Benedict might have had in mind not only John Paul but the Congress he inspired.

When we compare Pope Benedict's words in 2007 with those of John Paul II in 2002 at Lagiewniki, aren't the similarities in theme and content striking? John Paul II: "This fire of mercy needs to be passed on to the world." Benedict: "In our time, humanity needs a strong proclamation and witness of God's mercy. Beloved John Paul II ... prophetically intuited this urgent pastoral need." Connecting the dots, the world urgently needs God's mercy, and the Congress — inspired by John Paul II — was going to provide a means to further that aim in our time.

Was this an instance of Pope Benedict's "permanent dialogue" with John Paul II, which we covered in chapter one? Also, was Pope Benedict, so to speak, beginning to set the table for the Congress after conversing with his dear friend and predecessor about it? It's an intriguing thought.

At any rate, there is no doubt that on March 30, 2008, Divine Mercy Sunday — with the Congress only days away — Benedict began to set the table in earnest:

> In the coming days, on the occasion of the first World Apostolic Congress on

Divine Mercy, there will be a special reflection on Divine Mercy. It will be held in Rome and will begin with Holy Mass at which, please God, I shall preside on Wednesday morning, April 2, the third anniversary of the pious death of the Servant of God John Paul II. Let us place the Congress under the heavenly protection of Mary Most Holy, *Mater Misericordiae* (*Regina Caeli* message, the Second Sunday of Easter [Divine Mercy Sunday], March 30, 2008).

Notice how the Holy Father emphasizes that he will inaugurate the Congress by presiding at Holy Mass for the Servant of God John Paul II, on the third anniversary of his death. He states that at the Congress, "there will be a special reflection on Divine Mercy," pointing to how the Congress will delve into the mystery of God's mercy. Further, he invokes Mary's "heavenly protection" over the Congress under her title as the "Mother of Mercy" (*Mater Misericordiae*) — a title which refers to her special role in the mystery of Divine Mercy.

Inaugurating the Congress

Although more than 40,000 people gathered in St. Peter's Square on April 2, 2008, for Holy Mass on the third anniversary of the death of John Paul II, Pope Benedict in his homily singled out the nearly 4,000 delegates who were present for the opening of the World Mercy Congress:

> I address a special thought to the partici-
> pants of the first World Congress on
> Divine Mercy, which is opening this very
> day and which intends to deepen [John
> Paul II's] rich Magisterium on the subject.
> God's mercy, as he himself said, is a priv-
> ileged key to the interpretation of his
> Pontificate. He wanted the message of
> God's merciful love to be made known
> to all and urged the faithful to witness to
> it (cf. Homily at Krakow-Lagiewniki,
> August 17, 2002).

There are three interesting aspects to the Holy Father's remarks here. First, he says that one of the principal aims of the World Mercy Congress will be "to deepen" John Paul II's rich papal or magisterial teachings on the subject of God's mercy. Here, one thinks of Pope John Paul

II's second encyclical, *Dives in Misericordia* (*Rich in Mercy*), especially his insightful exposition of how the parable of the Prodigal Son reveals that God the Father is "rich in mercy."

Second, Benedict talks of how John Paul himself described God's mercy as "a privileged key to the interpretation of his Pontificate." In these remarks, Benedict may well be referring to Pope John Paul II's visit to the tomb of then Blessed Faustina at the Shrine of The Divine Mercy in Lagiewniki, Poland, on June 7, 1997.

During that visit, Pope John Paul II made these poignant remarks:

> I come here to commend the concerns of the Church and of humanity to the merciful Christ. On the threshold of the third millennium, I come to entrust to him once more my Petrine ministry — "Jesus, I trust in you!"

> The message of Divine Mercy has always been near and dear to me. It is as if history had inscribed it in the tragic experience of World War II. In those difficult years, it was *a particular support and an inexhaustible source of hope,* not only for the people of Krakow but for the entire

nation. This was also my personal experience, which I took with me to the See of
Peter and which in a sense forms the image
of this Pontificate (emphasis in original).

Third, Benedict is thinking of Pope John
Paul II's entrustment of the world to Divine
Mercy and his consecration of the International
Shrine in Lagiewniki in 2002 when he speaks of
how his predecessor "wanted the message of
God's merciful love to be made known to all and
urged the faithful to witness to it."

In fact, John Paul II stresses in his last sentence
before he makes his solemn entrustment: "May
you be witnesses to mercy!" He says these words
not only to "the Church in Krakow" but "to all
votaries [devotees] of Divine Mercy who will come
here from Poland and from throughout the world."

Interestingly, these emphatic words that call
us to witness to mercy set the stage for Benedict's
mandate, which we will explore in more depth in
our final chapter. Our goal will be to live the mandate, with Pope Benedict showing us the way.

Take the Initiative for Divine Mercy

But before we turn to our last chapter, let's
consider how Pope Benedict's example of encour-

aging WACOM and participating in it can inspire us in our own promotion of Divine Mercy. As we do, the key question for us becomes: What initiatives or projects for Divine Mercy can we pursue, given our own circumstances and gifts?

For me, one such initiative has been organizing a team to lead the "Three O'Clock Prayer" on weekdays at the Marian Helpers Center in Stockbridge, Massachusetts. This is one of the elements of The Divine Mercy message and devotion. It involves pausing to pray at 3 p.m. each day in remembrance of the hour Jesus died on the Cross. The hour is known and loved by Divine Mercy devotees as "the Hour of Great Mercy." Many pray the Chaplet of The Divine Mercy, while others pray the Stations of the Cross. Some spend the entire hour in Eucharistic Adoration.

Until several years ago, our longtime receptionist at the Center, Anne Myrick, had been leading the prayer, with me and other staff assisting her. Then, when she retired, I volunteered to lead and organize the prayer team.

On each weekday at 3 p.m., one of our team invites all the staff at the Center to stop at their workstations and pray. The prayer is spoken over the intercom system, and we pray a shortened version of the chaplet. We remember the intentions of those who, on that day, have contacted our Divine Mercy Prayer Line. We especially ask for courage and perseverance for the dying.

It also gives us the opportunity to share with our co-workers the encouraging news of answered prayers received by our prayer line staff and volunteers. One such answered prayer read, "After suffering two miscarriages, Beth Ann started to pray the Chaplet of The Divine Mercy. She wanted to let us know she just delivered healthy twin girls. Praise God!"

What about you? Is there some initiative for Divine Mercy that Jesus is prompting you to undertake in your family, neighborhood, parish, or at work? It may mean performing a work of mercy in your local community — for example, as a volunteer at a soup kitchen or through your local chapter of Habitat for Humanity, which builds affordable housing. Or if you are a Divine Mercy leader in your community, it could mean helping to organize a major event such as a Divine Mercy Sunday celebration in your area.

Take some time to pray about it and then entrust it to the Lord, saying, "Jesus, I trust in You!"

FULFILLING THE MANDATE

Our witness to God's mercy can be more effective if we focus our energy upon a particular initiative. Consider Pope Benedict's accomplishment. He blessed and encouraged the first World Apostolic Congress on Mercy in 2006. Benedict set the table for it with his strong remarks on Divine Mercy Sunday 2008, just days before it opened. Then he inaugurated the World Mercy Congress by celebrating Mass on April 2, 2008, for the Servant of God John Paul II on the third anniversary of his death. During his homily for the occasion, Benedict singled out the participants for WACOM, underscored their mission of deepening John Paul's "rich Magisterium" on God's mercy, and reminded them of how the Great Mercy Pope wanted everyone to know of God's merciful love and witness to it. Building on John Paul's legacy, Pope Benedict thus laid the groundwork for his own Divine Mercy mandate at the conclusion of the Congress.

Inspired by Pope Benedict, we are invited to consider how we can encourage and participate in projects that promote God's mercy in our own communities. It may be as simple as performing a work of mercy in our local community. Or it could be more involved such as planning a major event to promote Divine Mercy. Our personal prayer and trust in the Lord will be important in pursuing such an initiative. However the Lord leads us, may our witness to God's mercy bear good fruit.

CHAPTER NINE

Living the Divine Mercy Mandate

In our chapters, we've considered various ways that we can fulfill Pope Benedict's Divine Mercy mandate of going forth as "witnesses of God's mercy, a source of hope for every person and for the whole world." But what is most essential in our living the mandate? That is the question that we'll address in this chapter.

We can start by taking a deeper look at the context for the mandate at the first World Apostolic Congress on Mercy (WACOM).

Accenting Divine Mercy

First, for Pope Benedict, Divine Mercy is writ large in both his mandate and remarks on the Congress. Our witness to mercy must start with God and the mercy He provides.

It's telling that Pope Benedict, in all three of his statements about WACOM, used "Divine Mercy" in the title. He didn't use the name "World Apostolic Congress on *Mercy*" — the

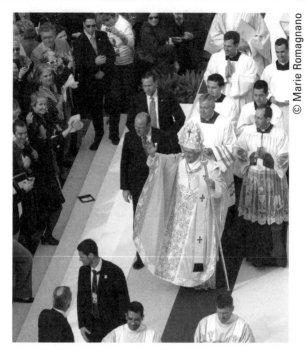

© Marie Romagnano

On April 20, 2008, Pope Benedict XVI greets the faithful at Yankee Stadium where he celebrated Holy Mass on the last day of his pastoral visit to the U.S.: "I was moved by his warm, gentle, and humble demeanor in celebrating Mass," said this book's author, David Came, who attended the papal Mass. "As he spoke, he put the merciful Christ forward and not himself. He was clearly an example of living mercy in our midst."

official title that the organizers developed to emphasize both the divine and human dimensions of mercy. In his *Regina Caeli* message on Divine Mercy Sunday, March 30, 2008, he referred to the Congress as the "first World Apostolic Congress on Divine Mercy." Then, during his homily at the opening Mass, he rendered the title "first World Congress on Divine Mercy." Finally, right before he gave his mandate on April 6 at the conclusion of the Congress, he put it this way in his *Regina Caeli* message: "Yes, dear friends, the first World Congress on Divine Mercy ended this morning with the Eucharistic Celebration in St. Peter's Basilica."

Further, notice that this use of Divine Mercy in the name of the Congress perfectly complements the wording for Pope Benedict's mandate. He tells us to "go forth and be witnesses of *God's* mercy," not our own human mercy. After all, with the mandate, it is God's mercy and not our own, which is "a source of hope for every person and for the whole world."

Here, Pope Benedict is not simply splitting hairs. He is clearly placing the emphasis on God's mercy toward us in our need, as the starting point. And it makes perfect sense since Benedict has always placed mercy — God's mercy — right at the heart of the paschal mystery, as we saw in chapter two. God in His mercy has taken the initiative in saving us through Christ. Our task is to trust in His mercy and be merciful to others ourselves.

This does not belittle human mercy at all. Remember Benedict's insightful image of the Good Samaritan being "struck in his soul by the lightning flash of mercy." Our mercy toward those in need is imperative, but it needs to flow from God's mercy and grace toward us to have staying power in our lives.

Cardinal Schönborn's Mandate

Along with this accent on Divine Mercy, it's helpful to realize another mandate was given on April 6, and it complements that of Pope Benedict.

The mandate was delivered by Cardinal Christoph Schönborn, who presented the idea for the Congress to Benedict in 2006. Now, on April 6, 2008, as president of the Congress, he was celebrating its closing Mass in St. Peter's Basilica.

First, let's hear Cardinal Schönborn's mandate. Then we will compare it to that of Pope Benedict.

"We are now departing after the blessed days of this Congress," he said in his homily, "and we are putting ourselves on the road with burning hearts to be everywhere and always with the Lord as witnesses of His immeasurable mercy." These words are the essence of the Cardinal's mandate.

He is referring to the Gospel for that Sunday, which is the account of the two disciples on the road to Emmaus from Luke 24:13-35. They are feeling dejected and disheartened after the crucifixion, until they meet Christ on the road. Then He opens their hearts to understand the Scriptures about the Messiah and how He had to suffer and die to enter into His glory.

The Lord begins to reignite their faith. They see He is in need of food and shelter. Through breaking bread with Him, they recognize He is the Risen Lord and make haste to spread the Good News, saying, "Were not our hearts burning [within us] while He spoke to us on the way and opened the scriptures to us?" (Lk 24:32).

"What an example for us, to prepare for our encounter with Christ through our hospitality," Cardinal Schönborn said, alluding to the disciples' hospitality toward Christ and their encounter with Him in Word and Sacrament. "'Be merciful as your Father is merciful.' How many times in living and performing simple works of mercy have we been able to experience the closeness of the Lord.

"The history of the success of Christianity is not a story of military triumphs or political triumphs," he continued. "It is rather the triumph of living mercy. Only in this way can you become convinced. The words can be beautiful, but in the end they are only words. But the acts of mercy, instead, are indisputable."

Now, let's compare the Cardinal's mandate with Pope Benedict's. First, note that just as Benedict called the participants to "go forth and be witnesses of God's mercy," so the Cardinal, in alluding to the Gospel account from Luke, calls them to put themselves "on the road with burning hearts to be everywhere and always with the Lord as witnesses of His immeasurable mercy."

As with Pope Benedict, the accent is clearly on being witnesses of *God's* mercy: in the Cardinal's words, witnesses of "*His* immeasurable mercy." But there is an added note of urgency to Cardinal Schönborn's words with the image of being "on the road with burning hearts." You get the sense, as with the disciples on the road to Emmaus, of being impelled to give witness because of a life-changing encounter with the

Risen Christ. So, too, recall how Pope Benedict challenged the youth of Poland and Germany as special witnesses of God's mercy to a personal encounter with Christ, as we saw in chapter seven.

Second, Cardinal Schönborn's mandate emphasizes performing works of mercy that flow from our experience of being close to the Lord. He describes such works of mercy as "the triumph of living mercy" that gives our witness credibility. Words are not enough. We've seen Benedict make the same kind of points about works of mercy in his reflections on the parable of the Good Samaritan in his book *Jesus of Nazareth* and in his first encyclical, *Deus Caritas Est (God Is Love)*. In his teaching, words are also not enough.

So what has this comparison gotten us? It has given a richness and a sharper focus to our discussion of Pope Benedict's mandate. We go forward in our witness to God's mercy with great zeal precisely because of a life-changing encounter with the Risen Christ. And our words are not enough. No, we are called to "the triumph of living mercy" by being merciful, because the Lord is so close to us in His great mercy.

The Pope and Cardinal after the Mandate

It's encouraging to report that after Pope Benedict delivered his own mandate on April 6, 2008, he had lunch with Cardinal Schönborn. Speaking to WACOM organizers later in a wrap-up session, the Cardinal said of the luncheon, "The Pope wanted to know all about the Congress." The Cardinal said he told the Pope that the Congress had been a great success, citing the presence of thousands of people from throughout the world who traveled to Rome despite great difficulties.

The Cardinal quoted the Pope as saying, "It is impressive to see Divine Mercy spreading through-out the world." He said Pope Benedict asked him to convey his personal thanks and blessing to all who were involved.

This account is drawn from the Summer 2008 issue of *Marian Helper* magazine, and it confirms the Pope's continuing interest in WACOM and the fulfillment of his own mandate.

'The Triumph of Living Mercy'

With this background in mind, then, what is most essential to our living Pope Benedict's Divine Mercy Mandate? We might sum it up as receiving the gift of Divine Mercy ourselves and then being merciful to others as "the triumph of living mercy" — to use Cardinal Schönborn's memorable expression. It's all about a life-changing encounter with the Risen Christ and then putting mercy into action ourselves by becoming men and women of mercy. Our witness is that simple and that profound.

Pope Benedict himself has shown us the way. As we've seen, he opened his heart to receive "a gift of Divine Mercy" at his election — through the intercession of John Paul II. At his 80th birthday, he also spoke of having received "a great gift of Divine Mercy" at his birth and Baptism. Clearly, he is close to Christ because he has had a profound experience of God's mercy in his own life.

This is precisely why he is able to be such a man of mercy and a Pope of mercy in fulfilling his Petrine ministry. He is a witness to "the triumph of living mercy." Consider, for example, how the media captured this dimension of Pope Benedict's ministry in their reporting on World Youth Day in Cologne, Germany, in 2005. As the well-respected German journalist Peter Seewald comments in his book *Pope Benedict XVI: Servant of the Truth:*

The World Youth Day gave great prominence above all to the humility of those who took part — and to the charism of the Holy Father. The Italian press commented: Now we are seeing a Pope who speaks of a loving and merciful God and of the Church as a "place of tenderness" (Ignatius Press, 2006, p. 168).

Here, remember how Pope Benedict invited the youth to draw near to the Eucharistic Christ present in the "Tabernacle of Mercy." He also encouraged them to be men and women of mercy like the Magi, who had had their own life-changing encounter with Christ, the newborn King.

Further, the editors of the *National Catholic Register* wrote in the editorial for their April 15, 2007, edition, which marked Divine Mercy Sunday that year:

> "God's passionate love for his people — for humanity — is at the same time a forgiving love. It is so great that it turns God against himself, his love against his justice."

This is a startling, radical statement about Divine Mercy — the kind of declaration that one might expect to be attributed to

Pope John Paul II. But it was Pope Benedict XVI who wrote it in his first encyclical, *Deus Caritas Est (God Is Love)*.

Seven years after Pope John Paul II first announced the creation of Mercy Sunday, many priests are still wary of the feast. Why do they hold back? There is a certain assumption that the Divine Mercy is a private devotion to a particular Polish man who happened to also be Pope, but that it is not for everyone.

Reading Pope Benedict's words about Divine Mercy should dispel that notion. Rather than attributing the popularity of the Divine Mercy devotion to Pope John Paul II, Pope Benedict seems more likely to attribute the greatness of Pope John Paul II to his devotion to Divine Mercy.

What a welcome surprise! A national Catholic newsweekly in the U.S. was noticing that Pope Benedict was himself a Pope of mercy. The editors were also pointing out how Benedict is saying that John Paul II's greatness stemmed from "his devotion to Divine Mercy." This insight is reminiscent of Pope Benedict's comment in an interview for Polish television in 2005 that John Paul II "created a new awareness of the greatness of Divine Mercy" as one of his main legacies. (We covered this in chapter one.)

It's interesting that while the *National Catholic Register* on April 15, 2007, and the Italian press at World Youth Day 2005 got it right in covering Pope Benedict, elsewhere the media point to the same reality in the Pope but don't call it "mercy." Seewald himself puts it this way in *Pope Benedict XVI: Servant of the Truth:* "[Benedict] surprises people by simply being himself: cheerful, warm, and humble" (p. 132).

In his booklet *10 Things Pope Benedict Wants You to Know,* Vatican correspondent John L. Allen, Jr., devotes an entire chapter to Benedict's extraordinary example of patience in a "microwave world." He also describes Benedict as "exceedingly humble and gentle" (Liguori Press, 2007, p. 44).

Whatever words we use to describe it, mercy is at the heart of Pope Benedict's appeal. His warmth, patience, humility, and gentleness reveal him to be a man of mercy, a Pope of mercy, who is encouraging us to embrace "the triumph of living mercy."

This was certainly my experience when I attended Pope Benedict's Mass at Yankee

Stadium on April 20, 2008, which came at the end of his pastoral visit to the U.S. It wasn't so much anything he said but who he showed himself to be by both his words and actions. I was moved by his warm, gentle, and humble demeanor in celebrating Mass. As he spoke, he put the merciful Christ forward and not himself. He was clearly an example of living mercy in our midst.

The Lesson for the Rest of Us

Now comes the hard part. This means our witness to God's mercy must have integrity if it is to be credible to the world. We must live mercifully every day and allow God's mercy to transform us into men and women of mercy. Then our world itself will, in turn, become transformed by "the triumph of living mercy."

It isn't enough to attend a World Mercy Congress or help organize a Divine Mercy Sunday celebration in our area. The Lord Jesus is calling us to a witness of mercy the Monday morning after and throughout the rest of our lives.

For me, it isn't enough to edit a magazine and books on Divine Mercy and now to write this book. I am called to be merciful every day with my wife and children — whether it's convenient or inconvenient. Even when I am on deadline at work for an important project and can tend to get "tunnel vision," I am called to see the needs of my co-workers, showing them mercy.

While this is challenging, Benedict has given us a program of mercy that can help us in pursuing this goal:

✝ We have each received a gift of Divine Mercy through our Baptism. The spiritual reality is that God in His great mercy has saved us through the Passion, death, and Resurrection of His Son, Jesus Christ. In fact, God's mercy is at the heart of the Gospel and our sacramental life as Catholics.

✝ Growing daily in trust in God is our foundational response to His great mercy toward us. It is our love, hope, and faith put into action.

✝ We are called to cultivate a trustworthy hope in God's mercy. Thus, we can go forth in great confidence as "witnesses of God's mercy, a source of hope for every person and for the whole world."

✝ God's mercy is intended for all sinners. It is not our place to judge the souls of particular sinners. We are called to plead God's mercy for them, praying that they would receive the grace of repentance.

✝ Like the heart of the Good Samaritan, our hearts should be disposed toward serving our neighbor in need. Such a disposition of the heart is best fostered by a prayerful and sacramental life.

✝ Whenever we are sick or suffer for any reason, we are called to trust in God's mercy and join our sufferings to those of Christ on the Cross. We should encourage the sick and suffering in our midst to do likewise.

✝ We are encouraged to pray for God's mercy for the dying and for the faithful departed. Such prayer is a powerful spiritual work of mercy for our brothers and sisters in need. While prayer for the dead isn't covered in any of our chapters, consider these words of Pope Benedict in his *Angelus* message for the commemoration of All Souls on

November 2, 2008: "Our lives are profoundly linked, one to the other, and the good and bad that each of us does always effects others too. Hence, the prayer of a pilgrim soul in the world can help another soul that is being purified after death. This is why the Church invites us to pray today for our beloved deceased and to pause at their tombs in the cemeteries." Prayer for the souls of the dead who may be undergoing purification in purgatory — especially offering the holy Sacrifice of the Mass for them — is particularly appropriate on All Souls Day and throughout the Church's monthlong November remembrance for the faithful departed. In the case of the dying, many of the faithful pray the Chaplet of The Divine Mercy at the bedside of the dying person. Jesus told St. Faustina that this is one of the best means of assisting the dying (see *Diary of St. Faustina*, 811 and 1541).

✝ Our youth are invited to an encounter with the merciful Christ in and through the Church. As they receive mercy from Christ, they are called to go forth into the world as young men and women of mercy. We should encourage them in this call.

✝ Our witness to God's mercy can be more effective if we focus our energy upon a particular initiative or project. Praying and trusting in the Lord will be important in pursuing such an initiative.

Working off this list, begin today to strive for "the triumph of living mercy." Go back and review particular chapters if it will help.

Remember that it all starts with us receiving God's mercy and then being merciful to others every day. Keep that as your baseline. As you do, keep your eyes on Pope Benedict. He is showing us the way, a way of mercy. It's his mandate, after all.

About the Author

David Came is the executive editor of *Marian Helper* magazine, the flagship publication of the Association of Marian Helpers, which is headquartered in Stockbridge, Massachusetts. He is also executive editor of Marian Press, which is the publishing house of the Marians of the Immaculate Conception located in Stockbridge. Came co-authored the Marian Press titles *Faustina, Saint for Our Times* and *Why Mercy Sunday?* with Fr. George W. Kosicki, CSB. He has written articles for the Marians' website www.thedivinemercy.org, including several on Pope Benedict XVI and Divine Mercy. Further, Came has edited numerous books and articles on Divine Mercy.

PROMOTING DIVINE MERCY SINCE 1941

Marian Press, the publishing apostolate of the Marian Fathers of the Immaculate Conception of the B.V.M., has published and distributed millions of religious books, magazines, and pamphlets that teach, encourage, and edify Catholics around the world. Our publications promote and support the ministry and spirituality of the Marians worldwide. Loyal to the Holy Father and to the teachings of the Catholic Church, the Marians fulfill their special mission by:

- Fostering devotion to Mary, the Immaculate Conception.

- Promoting The Divine Mercy message and devotion.

- Offering assistance to the dying and the deceased, especially the victims of war and disease.

- Promoting Christian knowledge, administering parishes, shrines, and conducting missions.

Based in Stockbridge, Mass., Marian Press is known as the publisher of the *Diary of Saint Maria Faustina Kowalska*, and the Marians are the leading authorities on The Divine Mercy message and devotion.

Stockbridge is also the home of the National Shrine of The Divine Mercy, the Association of Marian Helpers, and a destination for thousands of pilgrims each year.

Globally, the Marians' ministries also include missions in developing countries where the spiritual and material needs are enormous.

To learn more about the Marians, their spirituality, publications or ministries, visit **marian.org** or **thedivinemercy.org**, the Marians' website that is devoted exclusively to Divine Mercy.

SAINT MARIA FAUSTINA KOWALSKA

DIARY OF SAINT MARIA FAUSTINA KOWALSKA: DIVINE MERCY IN MY SOUL

LARGE PAPERBACK:
NBFD   9780944203040
768 pages, including 24 pages of color photographs, 5 ½" x 7 ¾".

COMPACT PAPERBACK:
DNBF   9781596141100
768 pages, including 24 pages of black and white photographs, 4" x 7".

DELUXE LEATHER-BOUND EDITION

Includes a special dedication from the Marians of the Immaculate Conception in commemoration of the first World Apostolic Congress on Mercy, gilded edges, a ribbon marker, and 20 pages of color photographs. 768 pages, 4 ⅜" x 7 ⅛".

BURGUNDY: DDBURG   9781596141896
NAVY BLUE: DDBLUE   9781596141902

AUDIO DIARY OF ST. FAUSTINA

You'll feel like you are actually listening to St. Faustina speak in a gentle Polish accent as she writes in her *Diary*. Hear this dramatic portrayal of the voices of Jesus and Our Lady. Gain deeper insight into Faustina's mission to share the message of Divine Mercy with the world. Includes all passages from the printed *Diary*, prayerful music, and 3 renditions of the Chaplet of The Divine Mercy. 33 hours on 27 CDs.

NEW!

ADCD
9781596142299